COMMUNICATIONAL MARKETING

Communicational Marketing

How to Communicate Effectively with
Competent Consumers

Luigi Carlo De Micco

iUniverse, Inc.
New York   Bloomington

Communicational Marketing
How to Communicate Effectively with Competent Consumers

Copyright © 2010 Luigi Carlo De Micco

iUniverse books may be ordered through booksellers or by contacting:

iUniverse
1663 Liberty Drive
Bloomington, IN 47403
www.iuniverse.com
1-800-Authors (1-800-288-4677)

Because of the dynamic nature of the Internet, any Web addresses or links contained in this book may have changed since publication and may no longer be valid. The views expressed in this work are solely those of the author and do not necessarily reflect the views of the publisher, and the publisher hereby disclaims any responsibility for them.

ISBN: 978-0-595-42867-0 (pbk)
ISBN: 978-0-595-68193-8 (cloth)
ISBN: 978-0-595-87205-3 (ebk)

Printed in the United States of America

Translated into English by Frederick S. Gardiner

iUniverse rev. date: 01/15/2010

For Monty Shadow and Polona

Contents

Acknowledgments

I would like to express my special gratitude to the following people and companies for providing me, in the course of numerous stimulating conversations, with many ideas and inspirations for this book: Alina Circu and her great family, Alessandro and Patrizia De Micco, Monty Shadow and his daughter Polona, Konstantin Stoyanov, Klaus-Peter Stoll, Wilhelm Seipel, Karin Alberts and Peter Lauster and the television broadcasting companies Pro 7, VOX, and RTL.

Preface

From Psychology to Communication: A New Approach

Successful marketing is characterized by a professional image, quality-conscious product management, and distinctive customer orientation. Although there is almost unanimous agreement about the entrepreneurial goals of marketing, the paths leading to these goals often vary considerably with respect to concepts and strategies. In the marketing practice of many enterprises and managers, the predominant approaches seem to based on increasingly complicated psychological and organizational theories and models. Nevertheless, all too often, even intensive efforts already fail in the early stages of implementation. For lack of results the good intentions are all that remain.

It is both astounding and amusing to watch the repeated spectacle of "great astonishment" and outright indignation when dedicated (and expensive) marketing strategists develop a fantastic (and, of course, expensive) concept, do a technically brilliant job of implementing it, only to end up at a loss to understand the reaction—or, rather, nonreaction—to it on the part of customers. During the mandatory discussions following such advertising flops, the blame is frequently given to the customers targeted: "They must have been too dumb to understand our fascinating offers and selling points...!"

Most advertising strategies are based in theory and method—that is, in the attempt to answer the question "How do I persuade the customer to buy my products?"—on psychological premises. Although many of these assumptions date back to the 1950s and 1960s, they are still applied today as if nothing has changed in the last forty years. The patent remedy is this: Just study how people think and then you will be able to infer how they make decisions. And once you know how your customers make decisions, you just need to provide a little assistance in order to give them what they want. The magic word for the study of these thought and decision-making processes is "psychology."

In the postwar years, people bought whatever they could afford. There was the "automobile boom," the "furniture boom," the "eating boom," and the "travel boom." Every product—regardless of how inane or expensive it was—had the chance of becoming a top seller. The main function of industry and business was to keep the supply line going. Economic theory concerned itself with developing strategies aimed primarily at optimizing production to try to keep up with the prevailing mass demand. In this ideal market situation of the postwar era, marketing was a simple affair. It was more concerned with introducing and demonstrating new products than with persuading people to buy them. From today's perspective, however, to ascribe the good sales results of the fifties and sixties to the advertising strategies employed at the time seems to be a doubtful thesis at best.

In spite of the recognition that market saturations inevitably occur and that these in turn bring about changes in consumer behavior, the principles of psychological marketing have remained unchanged. Techniques have indeed changed. The view of the target groups has also changed. With the use of modern media, effects can be realized that could only be dreamed of a few years ago. Everything has become more colorful, younger, faster, louder. But in the final analysis, the approach has remained governed by the precept mentioned above: just study how people think, and then you can draw conclusions about how they make decisions.

One could conclude that both then and now the question has been one of influencing people and their behavior. And in that case the most appropriate tool for analyzing people would seem to be advertising psychology—which, apart from a few minor adjustments, enjoys the same authority that it did forty years ago. Even if human behavior changed completely as a result of social, ethical, or market-related circumstances—so the thinking goes—these changes would not escape the psychology-oriented marketing strategist. For with its causal method, psychology ultimately registers and analyzes every change of behavior, to which the marketing strategy can then be adapted. After an analysis has been made of how and under what circumstances consumers make decisions, these psychological findings are employed in order to encourage the consumer to buy.

This sounds simple, logical, and easy to calculate. But, unfortunately, things do not work this way. In this book you shall learn why.

It seems an almost obvious tactic, but many companies never revisit existing marketing strategies to see if they should be revised against changes in consumer behavior. The technical implementation of marketing strategies has indeed changed in accordance with newly available media and the possibilities opened up by them, but this in itself does not exclude the possibility of miscalculating the market. And to this extent, the adaptation remains superficial and materialistic.

Example: If strategists in Germany start an advertising campaign to "make it clear" to customers that the new fee system of the German Telekom is better than the old one, although it results in a higher telephone bill for many customers, they shouldn't be surprised if this method meets with widespread disapproval, regardless of the impressiveness of the psychological and visual means employed. Not only will they throw a lot of money out the window, they will, as in this illustrative case, bring about a severe loss of image. (The advertising campaign of the German Telekom 1995–96 referred to here was finally halted by an interim injunction, whereupon the Telekom apologized in no less clumsy full-page advertisements).

The danger of "missing the mark" is also well illustrated by personnel marketing. In our increasingly individualized society, labor as a production factor is no longer understood in a narrowly functional manner. As a consequence of modern communication systems, with their faster channels of communication, greater demands are placed on individual employees. They are expected to make decisions as quickly and independently as possible. This brings about a new system of task allocation. A little over ten years ago, for example, data processing required primarily functions involving the simple acquisition of data. With the arrival of the personal computer and the Internet, data processing has developed into a dialogue system that makes fundamentally higher demands on individual employees and requires them to make decisions on their own. The difficulty arising from this lies in the unavoidability of a higher rate of error. Marketing experts can hardly cope with these difficulties even by means of the most skillful "personnel psychology."

This problem area is aggravated by obsolete organizational structures geared toward optimizing production. American and European companies are organized predominantly in a multitiered hierarchy that filters information from the bottom to the top. Of course, it seems to make good sense to shield the board of directors from "trivialities." But who decides what is unimportant? And how often does something get rejected at a higher executive level that was rated as a top priority at a lower level of the hierarchy? As a result of this institutionalized filtering system, one keeps hearing from top managers the following defensive statements: "No one told me about that"; "How are we supposed to know about that?"; "I don't work on the assembly line."

A good example is the experience of a management consultant working in a European automotive plant. Due to a windshield-wiper defect, a particular car model was showing an exceptionally high rate of failure to pass the final inspection. The defective cars had to be rerun through the production cycle, which resulted in enormous additional costs. When the consultant inquired about this, he learned from the responsible assembly-line worker that he had long been aware of the cause of the trouble. The problem was a small screw that was half an inch too short, causing the windshield-wiper mechanism to rotate. The consultant then went to the engineer in charge to inform him about this. The engineer noted the defect and referred to the company's suggestion-box system, for which explicit purpose a colorful box had been hung out. The consultant went back to the assembly-line worker and learned from him that he had repeatedly brought this defect to the attention of his foreman. However, he didn't want to drop a note into the box since he had already submitted a written suggestion on another occasion that had been dismissed because his spelling was found to be unsatisfactory. He was told he ought to take a language course.

Why did the employee act the way he did? Was it because of a psychological problem? Did he have too little self-confidence? Was he going through an identity crisis that could have been worked out in group therapy? Wrong! The problem was one of communication.

Here an important—a fundamental—item of information was rejected at the outset. In the industrial praxis of Western countries, remarks, suggestions, and market observations have to clear an average of ten hierarchical hurdles before they reach the responsible decision-maker. It is obvious that potential ideas, information, efficiency, and profit are getting lost along the way. Furthermore, the readiness to make suggestions is dampened because of a lack of response. In most cases, employees making suggestions get a response only if their suggestions can be technically and financially implemented— if they get any response at all. A token of recognition for trying to make a constructive contribution, as is customary in Japanese companies in the form of a short letter of thanks or a personal chat, is seldom provided for in Western companies.

Organization is good when the people implementing it are at the center of the model.

And how does one put people at the center of the organization, the marketing concept, the target-group definition, or for that matter at the center of any relationship? By using psychology? Wrong again! By means of communication.

In this book you will learn how communication functions and learn the laws that govern it. Concepts from psychology and psychoanalysis— e.g., subconscious, suggestion, trauma—have become an integral part of everyday language. Therefore, it is understandably difficult to depart from them for a moment. But precisely this is imperative for the understanding of communicational marketing.

Marketing comes into play whenever something is to be sold. Marketing lays out the course of action, determines the goals, and develops strategies by means of which these goals can be attained as quickly and effectively as possible. Ultimately, it is always a question of selling. Everyone, in the most various ways, is a seller. It doesn't matter if you are trying to get your friend to go to the movies with you, if you want to bring up your children to be good people, or if you are undertaking to convince your wife that you are a faithful husband. In all these situations, you are a seller, just like the nice gentleman at the front door who extols his vacuum cleaners, or a bank that tries everything under the sun to win back the confidence of its customers after a huge scandal.

Let us assume that as a rule our prospective customers don't need the things we offer them, and that they could well do without them. Here we are confronted with the problem of *convincing* them that they should buy them anyway.

A fundamental aspect of psychological marketing consists in analyzing the individual psychological laws governing human beings. Doing so examines human beings individually and in an artificial state of isolation. This "individualized analysis" of human behavior sounds good but the decisive error lies in the approach itself. In a therapeutic session it might well be appropriate to provoke the patient in order to make a diagnosis and analyze his or her psyche. After all, in psychotherapy the problems of individual persons are examined. In marketing, however, we are concerned with entire masses of people.

Nevertheless, individual methods and findings based on modern psychoanalytical research are taken over directly by advertising strategies without further ado. Some advertising campaigns even create the impression that they presuppose a customer profile with psychopathological features. The effective communication of advertising content, however, seldom addresses people with mental illnesses, and it is with this type of effective communication that marketing is concerned. It seems logical that the psychological approach doesn't work particularly well here.

Communicational marketing understands advertising, selling, and the attempt to convince as a communicative, dynamic process in which neither the behavior nor the psychological situation of the individual person occupies center stage. Communicational marketing considers it a fruitless undertaking to attempt to change the consciousness of entire masses of people by means of the psychological methods employed in the above-mentioned therapies for individuals.

Communicational marketing focuses on the processes that emerge *within intercommunicational relationships* and by which the behavior of the participants is lastingly influenced. These interpersonal processes take place to some extent independent of the respective psychological situations of the individuals involved. Thus, the sender of (advertising) information becomes, together with the opinion that the recipient has of the sender, part of the decision-making process and thus relevant to the behavior of the recipient. Communicational marketing presupposes a competent, self-directed buyer who categorically rejects suggestion and who is able to recognize manipulation whenever he or she is exposed to it.

Marketing means communication. To ignore the laws of communication means to run the risk of not reaching prospective customers—and certainly not by means of such a weak tool as advertising—even if the prospective customers are perhaps correctly understood from a psychoanalytical perspective.

In the following chapters, you will learn the fundamental laws of communication and how you yourself can make use of them to make more effective statements in advertising messages, career planning, or even within the context of your everyday relationships.

Part One describes how communication works. Much research has been done and much has already been written about the factors that determine people's behavior, as well as about how people can learn to understand themselves better.

The central question in the development of an advertising strategy, the formation a corporate identity, or even in the wording of an advertising message is this: "How can I convince my customer to buy my product?"

The general assumption is that it is easier to sell one's products to men or women if the typical psychological behavior of the respective individual or of entire target groups has been determined. As outlined at the beginning, this attempt is put in question here. Could it be that the approaches of every marketing department, every advertising agency, as well as entire branches of industry continue to make the same fatal error every day? This error owes its intractability to its pervasiveness, to its having become a habit, as it were. The result is a situation in which no one any longer dares to ask whether the wrong path might have been taken.

One thing does seem indisputable: in every attempt to get someone to do something—in this case to open up someone's pocketbook—communication takes place. It is not easy to demonstrate the applicability of psychological laws to every situation. The existence of communication, on the other hand, can invariably be demonstrated the moment it occurs. Therefore to effectively communicate advertising messages, it is essential to understand how communication really functions.

Part Two describes the practical effects of the communicational approach. Here you shall become acquainted with the various manifestations of communicational laws in interpersonal relationships and learn to better understand any number of various reactions.

Part Three focuses on entrepreneurial marketing—not from the classical psychological point of view, of course, but from the communicational perspective. The central issue is not the psyche of the individual,—as it is in hundred of books on marketing—but rather the salient mechanisms of communication.

Part 1

The Fundamentals of Communication

*Successful persons are those
who think up things
which the rest of the world then occupies itself with carrying out.*

—Don Marquis

Chapter 1:

A New Approach to Marketing

She:	"*You* love me!"
He:	"Yes!"
She:	"Do you love *me*?"
He:	"Yes!"
She:	"Do you *love* me?"
He:	"Yes!"
She:	"Do you *really* love me?"
He:	"Yes!"
She:	"I knew it! You *don't* love me!"

"Yes" means "yes" and "no" means "no"! That is what one would normally think, at any rate. Unfortunately, however, language by its very nature does not consist solely of unambiguous communications. Why is this the case? Whenever language is employed, whether in conversation or a formulated advertising message, we have verbal communication. In verbal communications, language is simply one element and does not depend solely on its defined codification and decodification.

If a computer carries out an order and delivers particular results, nobody thinks to ask, "What did it mean by that?" The human brain differs from a computer in its ability to assimilate almost unlimited amounts of data simultaneously. This characteristic of the unconscious assimilation of data and information is what makes human beings at once so interesting and so complicated.

Already several thousand years ago, people had started to study the medical factors of human existence that are quantifiable, empirically ascertainable. This was no doubt prompted by the pressing need to cure physical illnesses. The philosophers of antiquity had already started to describe a psyche that influences a person's thinking and behavior. However, research into the foundations of human behavior did not develop into the analytical science of psychoanalysis until the appearance of Freud in the nineteenth century.

The various modern marketing strategies, as well as all the seminars and courses on topics like rhetoric, sales, motivation, management training, success—of which the author has attended a considerable number—base their conceptions on the psychoanalysis of Sigmund Freud, if only partially and not seldom superficially. Virtually all of these seminars and courses start with a diagram of the "ego," "superego," and the "id" scribbled on a flip chart, which is then elucidated for hours on end. And this is done with the enthusiasm of reporting the latest evening news on CNN.

Freud can certainly be credited with enormous achievements and contributions regarding the modern conception of the human being. He set forth highly interesting theories for clinical practice and corrected a number of classical views about human behavior in the process. He provided many explanations and proposed numerous solutions that have retained their validity in modern psychotherapy to the present day.

The primary approach of psychoanalysis, however, is to describe the functioning and interrelationships of intrapsychic forces. Interactions among individuals, as well as their dependence on the environment, are left out almost entirely—most likely an intentional aspect of the therapeutical method. But despite the fact that psychoanalysis does construct a therapeutic basis by restricting its perspective to the individual, the forces in sociological constellations, and hence certain stimuli and forms of behavior, do not manifest themselves prior to the interaction among several individuals and are thus not amenable to the psychological approach.

This gap forms the starting point for the modern science of communication, which attempts to observe certain regularities in the interplay of these forces in order to interpret them scientifically. In this endeavor, communication science avails itself not only of psychoanalysis but also of a number of other disciplines, such as semiotics, rhetoric, syntactics, and semantics.

Communication is equated with behavior—that is, behavior among several individuals under certain environmental, personal, or situational conditions. Research in the field of communications focuses not only on why communications come about, but how and under what circumstances communications are assimilated and understood by their recipients. This is a very important aspect for the further discussion. The subject matter of the scientific study of communication is not so much the individual but rather the interpersonal transmitter-receiver constellation and its various manifestations.

To better understand the differences between the disciplines of communications and psychology, examine the chart below.

Communicational and Psychological Approaches		
	Central questions of the psychological approach	**Central questions of the communicational approach**
Approach:	The main focus is on individual human beings and their problems.	How does the behavior of the individual affect others?
Inquiry:	How do individuals relate to themselves? How do they understand themselves?	How is the psychological makeup of one's communication partner understood?
Procedure:	The causes of individual behavior (including pathologies) are sought for in the individual's psyche (childhood, traumas, etc.).	Behavior is studied on the basis of an interaction model as a reaction to the behavior of one's communication partner.
Behavior:	The behavior of human beings is primarily the result of their psychological makeup and hence of their anxieties and drives.	Behavior is subject to nonpsychological laws that manifest themselves apart from one's psychological state.
Illness:	The "mentally ill" person has an internal, self-related problem that manifests itself in "abnormal" behavior.	The inability to define one's own communication is causally connected with interpersonal problems.
Language:	Language is a tool for communicating one's intrapsychic state.	Language serves as *one* means of influencing one's communication partner.

Psychoanalysis deals with the relationship of the organism or individual psyche to its surroundings. Communication science, on the other hand, explains the manifold interrelationships in all their manifestations. Paul Watzlawick, one of the pioneers of communication science and himself a trained psychotherapist, employs a striking analogy to illustrate the contrast between the respective objectives of psychoanalysis and modern communication science.

If you take a walk and bump into a stone, energy from your foot will be transferred to the stone; the stone starts to roll and finally comes to rest at a place completely determined by such factors as the amount of energy transferred, the form and the weight of the stone, its surface characteristics, and so forth. If you bumped into a dog instead of stone, it might jump up and bite. In this case the relationship between the bump and the bite would be a fundamentally different one: the dog would undoubtedly make use of the energy of its own body and not that of the kick. What is transferred here is not energy but information.[1]

Let us return to the dialogue at the beginning of this chapter. We can draw a number of different conclusions from it.

1. The woman is crazy because she doesn't seem to *want* to understand that her husband really loves her.
2. The man is playing a nasty game with his partner. He does not, in fact, love her, but he won't admit it.
3. The woman does feel loved, but not enough (or not enough *today*).
4. The man and the woman *both* know that they have long ceased to love each other. However, the man doesn't want to say this out loud. The woman wants to finally clarify the situation.

You can certainly think of any number of other interpretations. If you knew the two people involved, you would, of course, find it easier to interpret the dialogue. But think back on similar situations: Could you always interpret a partner's dialogue accurately, especially in the heat of the moment?

The concepts considered in the following chapters, as well as the fundamentally different way of thinking employed, introduce thoroughly new aspects in modern marketing with respect to ways of evaluating, drawing conclusions, and taking action. To some extent these aspects run counter to marketing suppositions based on psychology and psychoanalysis. Marketing, advertising, and selling (as well as the entirely private personality management of individual executives or of a group in search of success) are, of course, also dependent to some extent on the intrapsychic situations of the individuals involved. Nevertheless, it will clearly be shown that communication and the laws governing it possess the greatest relevance for successful marketing.

---

[1] Watzlawick, Paul; Beavin, Janet H.; and Jackson, Don D. *Menschliche Kommunikation. Formen, Störungen, Paradoxien* ["Human communication: Forms, Disturbances, and Paradoxes"]. 8th printing. Verlag Hans Huber, 1990.

Chapter 2
Behavior: Innate or Learned?

Successful advertising and marketing influence behavior—the kind of behavior that occurs during a business transaction, in the formation of public opinion, in a lovers' quarrel, or in interpersonal conflicts. So we'll begin by examining the factors that influence human behavior. Wherein lie the origins and causes of the behavior that manifests itself on any given occasion? Psychologists, behavioral scientists, biologists, psychotherapists, as well as theologians—all are ready with their answers. We must briefly discuss two very contrary opinions reflected in marketing and advertising in many and varied forms.

One of the classical views of human behavior is the school of *behaviorism*. Its advocates start from the following premise: all human behavior is solely the result of environmental influences on the individual.

Behaviorists attempt to reduce the causes of human behavior to environmental influences alone—for example, by observing twins who have grown up in complete isolation from each other, who have never had contact with each other after birth and were brought up by different parents in different countries. Quite apparently, these twins developed in completely different ways as a result of their contrasting environments, in spite of having largely identical genetic "material." A further subject of observation has been the life history of the descendants of "genetically handicapped" criminals, who grew up to lead completely normal, noncriminal lives. Further experiments have been made with animals isolated from their parents in order to support the thesis that behavior is conditioned solely by an individual's environmental: these animals did not exhibit forms of behavior that had to be acquired by learning.

Over against the behaviorist view is the genetic approach established by Konrad Lorenz and numerous other biologists, social scientists, and ethnologists. This approach inspires equally absolute positions that

7

completely deny every environmental influence on human behavior and reduce all forms of human and animal behavior to genetic inheritance and its preprogramming.

The gestures, facial expressions, and other culturally conditioned forms of behavior of the most disparate peoples have been studied over the years by Irenäus Eibl-Eibesfeld, a student of Konrad Lorenz, in order to clarify the question of the causes of human behavior.[2] In some cases, these peoples could have never entered into contact with one another, which excludes the possibility of their having copied or learned anything from each other. Further substantiation of the genetic determination of behavior and entire patterns of interaction has been provided by observations and experiments concerning children born deaf and dumb. In the opinion of these scientists, if the thesis were tenable that all forms of behavior are the product of learning, then children who tragically had never had auditory or visual contact with their environment would exhibit no intelligible behavior.

The origins of behavior are certainly of great interest, with plausible arguments on both sides. If you were to now ask how communicational marketing views the origin of human behavior, I would reply with all brevity that it is a matter of complete indifference!

To attempt to determine the origins of behavior is to enter upon a speculative endeavor that can fill up large books and that may well be of the greatest significance for other disciplines. In marketing, however, such speculation won't help us create more successful advertising messages. For courses of action based on speculative suppositions must necessarily take on a speculative character themselves.

In marketing it is not infrequently the case that quite sizable budgets or even entire business enterprises are at stake. There is the risk of losing not only profits but also jobs and the livelihoods of those dependent on them. In essence, marketing is a question of business survival. To base entrepreneurial decisions—in which marketing plays a major role—exclusively on speculations would be to act irresponsibly. If, on the one hand, a manager miscalculates by making the wrong product decisions, a wrong cost estimate, or other miscalculations, he will have to live with the reproach of mismanagement, admit it to himself sooner or later, and hand in his resignation. If, on the other hand, millions of dollars are lavished on fruitless psychological frontal attacks for products that in the end no one wants to buy, then shareholders are shrugged off with the comment, "Sorry, the market wasn't ripe for our idea yet!"

---

[2]   Eibl-Eibesfeldt, Irenäus. *Der vorprogrammierte Mensch* ("The Preprogrammed Human Being"). dtv Wissenschaft, 1982.

Take the Corrado, Volkswagen's "top sports car." Corrados can still be seen occasionally. The advertising psychologists at VW identified a customer group of "financially weaker" Porsche fans and decided to provide them with an affordable alternative. In comparison tests, the Corrado repeatedly went up against the Porsche models 924 and 944. The Corrado came off pretty well thanks to its typical VW economy and its more favorable purchase price. The car proved to be a flop nevertheless. Only a couple thousand models were sold, and production was discontinued in 1995. The Corrado was no doubt a good vehicle technically; it combined sportiness with comfort, and at a tempting price. So where was the problem?

The marketing and product strategists at VW thought they had discovered a clear market niche that they could fill. The target group they identified consisted of people who like to drive fast while being economy-minded (gas consumption, maintenance, etc.). They identified the young, dynamic, self-confident entrepreneur who did not yet have the means for a "real" Porsche but who nevertheless wanted to emphasize his personal flair with a sports car. Perhaps the dynamic wife of the upper-income husband also fit into this group, a woman who would prefer to drive to the fitness studio with a Porsche but who was more likely to get an okay from her husband for a VW. Another likely candidate was the high school graduate who was supposed to get a sports car from his or her dad in order to be able to zoom off to the university with sporty yet economical flair, namely in a Volkswagen.

This strategy was thought up on the basis of psychologically analyzed and statistically substantiated data. It was a clear failure nonetheless. Why was this so? The problem was not the vehicle, nor was it the technology; it was not even the idea itself. The fault lay in the form of communication. The strategists fell victim to a fatally erroneous assumption: they thought they were able to precisely identify the target group and prognosticate its needs and behavior simply by subjecting it to a sufficiently intensive psychological analysis (their desires, fantasies, ideals, goals), fleshed out with a few nice statistics and survey results.

This is not to deny the existence of a very sizable segment of potential buyers who would like to have a sports car but who are not willing or able to spend the money. However, VW launched the Corrado as a direct rival product to the Porsche, an established "ideal in the area of sports cars," thereby sending the message (comparison tests, presentation, suggestions) of an "alternative." However, this claim was viewed by the targeted groups as a "phony alternative." In the consumers' mind-set, or *frame of reference* (to be discussed in detail below), "German sports car" is associated with "Porsche" and not with "Volkswagen," just as "German luxury car" is associated with "Mercedes." The Volkswagen brand, on the other hand, is associated with economy, solidity, and "quality at a low initial cost." You shall learn in this book that the attempt to influence consumers by means of suggestive advertising not only *fails* to convince them but also *prejudices them against* the originator of the advertising message.

Thus, in this case, Volkswagen probably underestimated the effect of its own communication. It is perfectly legitimate to formulate an alternative. If the alternative is not "genuine," however, consumers cannot be induced to accept it. The alternative then becomes a poor compromise, and whose interest is piqued by something like that?

Now, what do you think VW gave as reasons for the production stop? Technical problems, sales difficulties, high development costs, high production costs, high wage levels, increasing fringe benefits, etc.

Where was the research on communication?

To be sure, every good business decision does require a little bit of luck. However, this shouldn't be taken to mean that marketing is only a matter of luck. The sums at stake are simply too high.

Let us now have a look at the practical foundations of communication.

Chapter 3
Axioms of Communication

Some of the findings of modern communication science are themselves results of clinical studies in psychiatry, psychotherapy, and psychoanalysis. Various scientists involved in therapy and psychoanalysis have recognized that psychological problems don't always have to be solely the product of intrapsychic modalities (childhood, sexuality, aggression, anxieties, etc.). These scientists were able to transcend the mind-set acquired during their primary, somewhat dogmatized education and began to study behavior in human communication. The subject matter of their work was no longer the "hermetic room of the psyche" in which "patients" confront themselves, define and understand themselves in relation to their environment, and seek explanations within themselves for conflicts, depressions or pathologies.

It was then possible to find in "nonpsychic space" other causes for forms of human behavior—causes that are governed by other kinds of laws. This nonindividualistic dimension is the sphere of communication.

As a result of these practical studies, some "pragmatic axioms" were formulated. These axioms give clear formulation to fundamental laws in the analysis of communication. Paul Watzlawick describes the axioms as "provisional formulations that can lay claim neither to completeness nor finality." These fundamentals of communicational behavior have proven to be quite useful in the practical study of human behavior in all its various manifestations. They facilitate the understanding of many forms of interaction and hence of problems in daily relationships.

In the following you will become acquainted with some of these axioms. Remember these axioms if you find yourself developing a marketing strategy for your product, your enterprise, or your personal career; some of the rules of the game are laid down by communication, the disregard of which can result in losing the game.

Axiom No.1: It Is Impossible to Not Communicate.

To communicate means to act in a certain way.

Any given instance of communication is a manifestation of a behavior that conveys information. This behavior can manifest itself in a great variety of ways: speaking, remaining silent, writing, brooding, sighing, laughing, refraining from laughing (although everyone else is laughing), pausing while speaking, gesturing, changing expression, using body language, getting up and leaving, and so on. Consider a conventional conversation between two persons: the person is communicating who at the moment is speaking, calling, yelling, writing; he or she is expressing something. As soon as the communication becomes reciprocal, an interaction takes place. Interaction requires at least one reaction that is registered by the other person.

Behavior has this fundamental characteristic: it has no converse. Nobody can claim that they wouldn't behave in any way in a given situation or at a given place. Remaining silent, watching without comment, or ignoring something are also forms of behavior. Consider the political stance of some countries in the most recent Balkan conflict. Apparently, some politicians thought they could avoid taking part in the intense debate by remaining silent, not making any commentaries, or by making it clear that they "wanted to stay out of it." All these were certainly forms of behavior. Their behavior was perhaps even more telling than that of those who openly and emphatically condemned the war in the Balkans and the actions of the Serbians.

What follows is that it is impossible to refrain from behaving. Now, if every form of behavior by which something is imparted is communication, then it is impossible not to communicate. The practical consequences of this characteristic of behavior are far-reaching. For it is equally impossible for the recipient of an item of communication not to react. Reacting consists therefore in a form of behavior in which the recipient communicates on his or her part.

Communication is generally connected with audible sounds or visible gestures. Thus it can be difficult to grasp that passivity and nonreaction are also indicative of communication.

Everyone is familiar with the situation in a waiting room. Two or more persons sit across from each other. Each person is aware of the presence of the other or others, but no one acknowledges the presence of anyone else. Eye contact is avoided. If someone coughs, no one gives any indication of having noticed. You will agree that communication nevertheless takes place in such a situation. What is signaled is: "I want to be left in peace," or "I am not interested in having a conversation." If such silent behavior is verbalized interpretively, possible statements can be formulated—which provides evidence of communication.

This situation of "passive communication" in a waiting room usually comes to an end without any particular consequences. At some point, the situation just ceases to exist; one person after the other leaves the room, perhaps with a scarcely audible "Good-bye." If there are no personal interests among the persons involved, it would not occur to anyone to interpret this situation as some kind of grand refusal to communicate.

The behavior of passive communication or the attempt to avoid communication can have tragic consequences in relationships, however, for in these situations the attempt is always made in one way or the other not only to take notice of the behavior but also to interpret it. A company that fails to react to the complaint of a customer informs him or her by this behavior that the customer is a matter of indifference. In this case the company does nothing. Not even physical proximity, as in our waiting room, obtains in this instance of communication. Nevertheless, the company was communicating here in a manner that was unambiguous for the customer.

This example alone makes clear the high degree of importance passive communications can have for the analysis of entrepreneurial behavior. The attempt to avoid communicating generally gives rise to suspicion (here between enterprise and customer). At the very least, it provides an occasion for speculation. Time and again, chemical corporations get entangled in environmental scandals or politicians are accused of "irregularities." One reaction is: "No comment. I am innocent and therefore I do not have to defend myself!" This form of behavior leads to an even greater loss of credibility, despite the fact that the parties keeping silent have done nothing to directly incriminate themselves. When formulating advertising messages, therefore, the attempt should never be made to "not communicate." Such attempts have fatal consequences.

Axiom No. 2: Communication Has Informational and Relational Aspects.

Information is communicated by such means as news reports, memos, and notes. At first, this sounds simple and straightforward. Taken by itself, an item of information can be true or false, important or unimportant, elementary or trivial. Pure information is a neutral, factual matter. It can be accepted, declined, or ignored.

Information describes the *matter-of-fact, content aspect* of an item of communication. This aspect is also called the *factual level* or the *objective level*.

The statement, "The weather is so beautiful today," is a clear, trivial observation about the weather with an unequivocally informational character.

In addition to the factual, informational aspect, every communication contains a further characteristic that is not so apparent. This second aspect imparts *the way in which the communicator wants his information to be understood by the recipient.* By this means, the communicator defines not only the isolated item of information; he also defines the *relationship* to the recipient, or what he understands this relationship to be. We call this area, in which information about the communication is conveyed, *the relational level.*

Communication Model

Because this plays out in almost every form of communicational behavior, this axiom has to be regarded as one of the most important. If not for the factual and relational aspects of communication, then the notorious misunderstandings that arise in conversations, negotiations, and discussions would not occur. All communication would be unequivocal, and people would have considerably fewer problems.

It is important to note that every communication is characterized by two levels: the level of (matter-of-fact) information and the level of information about this information. The content or informational level conveys data; the relational level defines how these data are to be understood. In every single type of communication, the relational aspects dominate; they stand above the informational level, as it were, and determine it. The relational aspects are therefore assigned to the sphere of "metacommunication."

Let us return to the harmless statement mentioned at the beginning, "The weather is so beautiful today." Now imagine that this remark comes at Sunday breakfast from a wife who has been trying for months to get her uninterested husband to go for a Sunday walk with her. This harmless observation suddenly acquires a completely new character. Depending on the events leading up to this interaction, one could imagine that on that particular occasion the wife didn't want to directly suggest—i.e., at the content or informational level—taking the long-awaited Sunday walk. Or perhaps all she wanted to do was simply start off the breakfast conversation in a friendly manner with the pleasant remark "The weather is so beautiful today."

The husband, who is not exactly thrilled about Sunday walks, registers the apparently pleasant and friendly remark of his wife quite differently and immediately associates it with an entire chain of presumptuous provocations: "You never go for a walk with me"; "I don't dare to ask you to take a walk with me anymore"; "In fact, I don't dare to ask you anything anymore"; "And besides, you don't want to do anything with me anymore, anyway"; and finally, "You don't love me anymore!"

We can also put the shoe on the other foot: The husband mentions the nice weather to his wife, who is definitely not the athletic type, and she associates "nice weather" with a bicycle tour her husband has long been wanting to take.

Both cases make clear the enormous consequences of this characteristic of human communication. Particularly interestingly in this respect is the fact that *the relational aspect of communication usually dominates over the informational aspect!*

The dominance of the relational aspect the informational aspect can manifest itself in myriad ways. This makes the relational aspect of communication extremely complex. A high-risk potential lurks here for unintentional complications and "misunderstandings," which can turn into real problems. We are all familiar with remarks like, "I didn't mean it that way," or "That's what I thought it meant."

On the other hand, the existence of the informational and relational aspects in communication also provides powerful instruments for the strategic placement of information. Let us assume a successful attempt has been made at formulating a communication (informational aspect) in which the recipient's manner of interpretation (relational aspect) is known to the communicator. This makes it possible for the communicator to influence the recipient more easily. For the dominance of the relational level also means that conclusions drawn at this level are judged to be "true" by the recipient.

An example: Assume that you want to convey to your customer that your product is particularly long-lasting. In this case, it is not advisable from the communicational view to formulate this explicitly, namely by saying, "Our products are particularly long-lasting." To say this is to create the ideal conditions for the most exotic interpretations. Such formulations lead to exactly the opposite of what was originally intended. We will examine the reasons for this later on. Additionally, customers might hold suspect your company's own claims as to the durability of its product.

Paul Watzlawick clarifies the axiom of the informational and relational aspects of communication in the following example.

> A man is held prisoner in a room by two guards. The room has two exits. Both doors are closed but only one is locked, and the prisoner does not know which one. The prisoner knows that one of the guards always says the truth, whereas the other one always lies. However, he doesn't know which one of them is the liar. In order to escape, he has to successfully accomplish the following task: Find out which of the two doors isn't locked by putting a single question to one of the two guards.

> Our prisoner has only one sure possibility of solving the puzzle. If he were to ask one of the guards willy-nilly which door was locked or unlocked, he could only guess whether the guard he addressed was lying or telling the truth. The prisoner knows merely that one of the two guards lies and one tells the truth. He can liberate himself only by moving onto the metalevel. He has to speak to an arbitrarily chosen guard and make a reference to one or the other of the two doors:

> "If I were to ask your comrade whether this door is open, what would he say?" If the answer is "No," then this door would be the unlocked door; in the case of a "Yes," the prisoner ought to choose the other door.

It shall be left up to the reader to think through this solution. What it basically involves is a double negation, a law of logic. The prerequisite, of course, is that both guards know that the other behaves in a complementary fashion.

Depending on the form and modality of the relationship in question, the dominance of the relational aspect can be very extensive. This dominance can relativize the informational aspects of an item of communication to the point of irrelevance. From this state of affairs, the following conclusion can be drawn, which obtains for information in advertising as well: Under certain circumstances, it is completely irrelevant what is said, written, or portrayed visually. What counts is *how the communication comes across to the person being addressed.*

Axiom No. 3: All Communication Has a Digital and an Analog Aspect.

In a manner comparable with electronics and mechanics, digital and analogous characteristics can be demonstrated in communication as well. Electronic digital transfer is characterized by a particular language. In EDP, digital language is expressed by the ciphers 1 and 0 (yes/no; in/out). By means of their manifold possibilities of combination in varying series and sequences, they constitute an unequivocal code for more complex results.

A similar situation exists in human communication. There are two fundamentally different means by which objects or states of affairs can be represented and thus rendered communicable. They can either be expressed by an analogy (e.g., a diagram) or by digitalization, a name, or a designation. These two possibilities of expression correspond to the above-mentioned analogous and digital forms of communication in artificial organisms (computers). As a rule, the names and concepts we use are verbal constructs whose relation to the object thus described are purely coincidental or arbitrary. There is no compelling reason, for example, why the three letters "d," "o," and "g" in this order should designate a certain animal. This relationship between word and object is based simply on a semantic convention. Apart from such conventions, which to some extent are culturally conditioned, there is no further relationship between a word and what the word designates.

In analogous communication, on the other hand, a certain kind of objectivity can be ascertained in the expression used for the description of an object or a condition. The word "analogy" means the manifestation of a certain resemblance to the object for which the expression stands.

The difference between digital and analogous communication becomes even more clear if one reflects on the fact that simply hearing an unknown language never can result in understanding that language. However, the interpretation of accompanying gestures in foreign languages and cultures (analogous communication) leads to the understanding of many communications without first having to a gain a mastery of the language.

On the basis of the characteristics of the two forms of expression described here, it can easily be understood that at the object level (see second axiom) digital communication primarily takes place. The relational level, on the other hand, is characterized by analogous communications.

These classifications may still seem somewhat theoretical at this point, but they will prove very important for the further discussion of communication.

Axiom No. 4: Interactions Can Be Symmetrical and/or Complementary.

Interaction is defined in reciprocal communication, i.e., *intercommunication*. This means that the "receiver" will react in one form or another to the communication of a "transmitter." In accordance with the axiom of the impossibility of not communicating, such a reaction can also take place in the form of an apparent nonreaction (such as ignoring the action).

In the observation of all the various forms of interaction (between partners, social groups, enterprise and customers, or between nationalities, etc.) certain intercommunicative patterns can be clearly discerned. A certain type of dominance obtains in the behavior of the respective parties involved.

Participants in a process of communication are involved in a process of differentiation with respect to the parameters, or norms, defining the reciprocity of the relationship. This means that they tend to define both their own respective position and that of the other participant at times in general terms and at times in situational terms. Consider how consumers assess companies to discern the veracity of their marketing claims, just as companies analyze the responses of consumers who participate in survey and focus groups. This leads to very different forms of interaction. Interactions have the characteristic of taking place on either a symmetrical or complementary basis.

A symmetrical interaction is based on equality. A high degree of agitation on the one side, for example, is countered by a similar amount of agitation on the other side. If one intercommunicator behaves in a more quiet or calm manner, the other reacts in an analogous manner.

In a complementary process of interaction, the behavior of the one participant complements—i.e., confirms or reinforces—that of the other. Symmetrical interaction, on the other hand, is based on the striving for "identity" and the (reciprocal) reduction of, and disregard for, features that distinguish the interlocutors from one another. Complementary interactions have the opposite tendency of reciprocally confirming and sometimes even strengthening the differences between the communicants.

Complementary patterns of interaction take place whenever the participants are distinguished from each other by two fundamentally different initial positions, whereby one of the participants occupies the superior position and the other the inferior position. The pertinent question here is whether the dominating position can change in the course an interaction between the communicants. In determining the positions of superiority and inferiority, the attempt should be avoided to try to evaluate the situation objectively— i.e., to infer the structure of dominance from judgments about the rightness, strength, or relevance of the statements of the respective parties. In our observations, the superior or inferior position of the intercommunicators does not depend on the quality of the individual statements. Complementary and symmetrical forms of interaction are defined to a much greater extent by cultural, sociological, or economic constellations, such as the relationships customer-seller, teacher-pupil, or father-son.

For the analyses of communication in marketing, as well as for the development of instruments for the effective conveyance of advertising messages, a further overarching pattern of interaction is relevant, namely the *metasymmetrical and metacomplementary level of interaction.*

At this level, the metainteractive intercommunicator consciously accords, by words or actions, a certain position (primary or secondary) to the receiver of his messages. By intentionally putting himself in a complementary or symmetrical position, he can by this means influence the interaction at the metacommunicative level. However, this works only as long as the "naive intercommunicator" doesn't recognize the situation for what it is. As soon as he sees through the metainteraction of the other intercommunicator, for example by a revealing remark at the relational level, the strategy loses its effect and the tables can very quickly be turned. If the recipient becomes aware of the fact that he was accorded the dominant role simply in an instrumental sense, say, in order to be more easily manipulated, he will interpret this behavior as an attack and will adopt a defensive stance.

In summary, the axioms of communication have shown us the following:

- Every communication can be examined in terms of the laws governing it.

- In certain situations it is impossible not to communicate—namely whenever at least two individuals capable of communicating encounter each other in any context or avail themselves of media in order to communicate with each other. As soon as two persons enter into contact with each other, there is always at least one person who sends out signals while the other person receives them.

- Every communication is characterized by an informational level and a relational level. The expressive power of the relational message usually dominates, for it is processed in the mind of the recipient and therefore in an entirely subjective manner.

- Interactions can take place on a symmetrical or a complementary basis. Symmetrical interaction is based on the mutual striving for equality. Complementary interaction is characterized by the reciprocal reinforcement of the primary or secondary position of one's communication partner.

- The informational aspect of communication (language, written text, code), is communicated digitally; the relational aspect (gestures, facial expression, pictures) is communicated analogously.

In advertising, we know of numerous examples of metainteractive patterns that are prone to fail because of the mechanism just described. The effect can be easily observed in a company's attempt to generate a higher degree of credibility and thus a greater readiness of their consumers to buy. Such a company does a meticulous job of defining target groups. In detailed studies, the social, cultural, financial, or occupational similarities of prospective buyers are researched, and empirically substantiated "classes of buyers" are determined. These classes are then copied straight into the advertising messages. The advertising psychologist hopes to thereby obtain a higher identification effect from the target group, which will in turn lead to higher credibility. That might be true and might even work up to a certain point.

But what happens if the target group catches on to the purpose of the exercise? What if the misfortune occurs that consumers, who have obviously been classified as extremely naive, catch on to the fact that they, or their behavior or social context, has been copied for the purpose of creating a pseudoidentification?

Those persons being addressed by the advertising message will then feel manipulated and react defensively. And the goal of obtaining a greater readiness to buy based on higher credibility disappears down the drain. And the splendid psychological model collapses like a house of cards.

Chapter 4
The Pitfalls of Interaction

A basic element of (and form of expression in) communication is *interaction*. Interaction is constituted by an accumulation of communicational units and events—e.g., a questioning look, a verbal reply, passing by someone without a word. To the extent that occurrences of communication are related to each other, we speak of the *punctuation of the sequences of events*. An example: He went away after he told her off. She angrily slammed the door behind him ...

Interaction

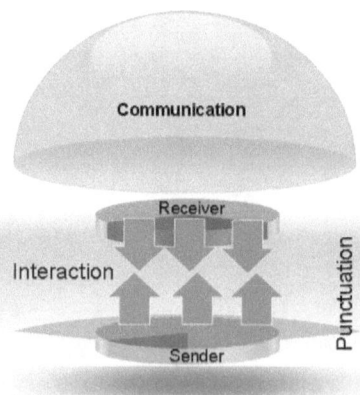

Stimulus-response psychologists concentrate their attention primarily on reciprocal behavioral sequences that are so brief that these psychologists designate the one event as the stimulus and the other as reinforcement. The behavior between these two events exhibited by laboratory animals is then defined as the response. Within the bounds of a narrowly restricted, determined sequence, which makes the laboratory experiment possible, it seems plausible to speak of a "psychology of the laboratory animal."

By contrast, the sequences in human communication are not only substantially longer, they are further distinguished by the characteristic that each and every event can at once be a stimulus, a response, and a reinforcement.

In any marketing interaction, the behavior of a seller is a stimulus inasmuch as it is followed by some kind of behavior on the part of the customer, which is in turn followed by some kind of behavior on the part of the seller. The behavior of the seller is also a response inasmuch as it is embedded between two forms of behavior on the part of the buyer. However, the behavior of the seller is also a reinforcement, since it follows upon an action of the buyer. Thus, the interaction arising here is a chain of triadic members of which every single one can be regarded as a stimulus, a response, or reinforcement.

As described in Axiom No. 4, it makes no difference whether the punctuation is good or bad, meaningful or not, logical or even paradoxical. All that matters is that the respective item of punctuation helps to organize behavior.

The fact of being part of any given culture involves very specific, indigenous forms of interaction that require respectively "appropriate" behavior. Deviations from these communicative norms give rise to misunderstandings—in the truest sense of the word—and consequently to problems.

This provides a possible explanation for the antipathies toward other ethnic groups or peoples which can be found to a lesser or greater degree in all countries on earth. The reason for such intolerance and chauvinistic behavior toward others on the part of entire nations frequently has little to do with factual issues or with religious or political and ideological differences; the cause is often rooted quite simply in a totally different form of communication.

It follows that it should be of great relevance for the formulation of advertising texts to know how communication works and what its normative structures are.

Anthony Robbins is an American coach for executives and sellers who, with a high degree of rhetorical skill, conducts successful seminars all over the world with over three thousand participants. He illustrates this aspect of the different forms of interaction by means of a telling experience.

In his somewhat demagogic lectures, Robbins makes considerable use of theatrical body language. During a seminar in Venezuela he tried to reinforce a provocative thesis, which he kept on repeating, by firmly clapping the palms of his hands together. In most industrial countries, clapping one's hands together is considered to be a reinforcing instrument that emphasizes a statement. In Venezuela, however, this gesture is regarded as an unambiguously vulgar sexual proposition. Not until he learned the digital meaning in Venezuela of his gestures did it become clear to Robbins why he was able to elicit no approval for his proposals from his audience but only a shocked reaction.

The Pattern of Interaction in Role-Playing

As has been shown in Axiom No. 4, two fundamental role types can repeatedly be observed in every interaction: leader and follower. In the course of the interaction—and this is the exciting part—these roles can be reversed. The role assignment, therefore, is relative.

Sociologically determined role phenomena characteristic of families (father-son, mother-father) and other social groups do not have to be assumed in every interaction. It is more a question of the relative position at any given juncture. Certain regularities are also exhibited by the positions of communicants involved in interactions in which both parties can be complete strangers, ones in which the respective social status is at first unknown.

In practice it is very difficult to determine which of any two communicants occupies the dominant position, and what the one "role type" would be like without the presence of the other participant. Most interpersonal conflicts— whether in sales talks, during the transmission of advertising messages, in marriages, or wherever—seem to stem from differences arising in the respective interaction.

Let us consider the following example of a marriage situation: An interpersonal problem can arise because the husband adopts an essentially passive and withdrawn stance, while the wife—from the point of view of her husband—has an exaggerated tendency to complain. The husband, who keeps on insisting how very much he loves his wife, explains that his stance is the only possible defense against the constant complaining and criticism of his wife. He is convinced that more activity on his part would only reinforce the complaining of his wife and all the ensuing discussions. The wife, on the other hand, who continually avows how very much she loves her husband, maintains that the sole cause of her criticism is the behavior of her husband, who withdraws from her with his passivity.

Both perceive their own behavior as a response to that of the other. This is a typical interaction model which most everyone has experienced in some form or another.

A psychoanalytical attempt at solving this interpersonal problem would probably start with the isolated causal analysis of the behavior of each party involved. A therapist who is not communication-oriented would delve deep into the subconscious of the wife described above, searching for hidden phobias, childhood experiences, or sexual delusions to explain the woman's aggressive behavior toward her husband. The next step (after perhaps two years of intensive consultation) would be to combat these intrapsychic causes with all the various therapeutic methods. Similar treatment could lie in store for the husband, but here with the result that "at bottom, he accepts and loves only his mother as the woman in his life but is, in fact, more homosexually oriented or has simply developed an anxiety neurosis about women or ..."

Such interpersonal conflicts could be solved if the parties were put in a position to metacommunicate—that is, to communicate about their own interaction, for it is here that the real cause of the problem lies, at least in the above case.

Interpersonal differences of opinion that arise with respect to matters of fact, taste, or opinion should be viewed as easy-to-solve difficulties. A real problem arises only by using the false approach with which one hopes to solve the (relatively unproblematic) difficulty. Then the solution itself turns into the real problem. That is the way it is with human communication.

One may discover repeatedly, by interviewing company employees and their customers, that far-reaching disagreements about all kinds of details can dominate common experiences and transactions between the two parties. Sometimes the two parties may seem to inhabit different worlds or not to be speaking about the other party at all. Here as well the problem lies in the inability to engage in metacommunication. This inability turns their interaction into an unrelenting "yes-no-yes-no-yes-no oscillation," which theoretically can go on forever, or up to the point when the customer gets fed up and quits. When such situations spin out of control, this oscillation inevitably leads to stereotype accusations and counteraccusations of willfulness, profit greed, malice, or even insanity.

This phenomenon can also be frequently observed in relationships between nations. One needs only to recall the arms-race madness of the 1980s or all the ethnic disputes that continue to this day—disputes in which one can no longer determine the cause or identify the initial aggressor: "Everything was started sometime by someone ..." Each of the parties involved is convinced that it never did anything but react. All the parties view themselves as victims who have simply defended themselves by hitting back with the same means employed against them.

Can you remember your last argument with your spouse or with a customer? Wouldn't you swear to it that it was the other party who started everything with his or her behavior?

Consider the following points about the pattern of interaction in role-playing.

- The nature of a relationship is defined by the way the communication processes are punctuated by the parties involved.
- The informational aspects can complement each other or completely contradict each other.
- Every interaction is subject to certain laws that can manifest themselves to a greater or lesser degree depending on the given sociocultural situation.
- Interaction takes place at both the digital and the analogous levels. Interactions define the form and the course of the communication.

In the following chapters, it will become even clearer that precisely in advertising it makes virtually no difference what is said or written. What counts is how the message is received by the person or persons being addressed.

Chapter 5
The Problem of the Religious Scientist

Human behavior in all its expressions and manifestations is an extremely complicated, complex, and interdependent matter. Many highly intelligent and thoughtful minds have capitulated before now in the famed search for an "all-encompassing" explanation.

Only the religions seem to be able to offer acceptable and—above all—comprehensible explanations. The reason for this is that, contrary to scientific methodology, they obviate the necessity of proof by simply accepting human imperfection and believing in the existence of a higher being who perhaps guides human affairs. Religious faith simply does not need any proofs. For scientific knowledge, on the other hand, proof is an indispensable support of the intellectual attempt to grasp complex relationships.

It follows that between religion and science not only debates about fundamentals are pointless. Equally pointless is the reciprocal assessment of all of the decision-making processes based either on scientific grounds, on the one hand, or on religious faith, on the other—for the respective underlying paradigms are fundamentally different.

Let us take as an example the "discussion" between a proponent of the Darwinistic theory of evolution and a member of the Jehovah's Witnesses. By means of "rigorous scientific proofs," the Darwinist casts doubts on the depiction in Genesis and on the figures of Adam and Eve. The Jehovah's Witness, on the other hand, believes unreservedly in the literal existence of the biblical figures. It is readily apparent that this discussion will never arrive at a satisfactory conclusion. This communicational dilemma is based on different, apparently contradictory, premises. This dilemma expressed itself in its most glaring form by the practices of torture and the burning of witches in the Spanish Inquisition in the Middle Ages .

But how then can a natural scientist, who explains the origin of the world by means of modern techniques, such as the ascertainment of half-lives, genetic engineering, and molecular analysis, be a believing Christian? This is a fair question in the light of the obvious contrast to religious premises.

With respect to the question of the definition of proof, the religious natural scientist is able to keep separate and accept both points of view—at a metalevel. This enables him or her to reflect on the nature of communication itself. The religious scientist understands that the digital notion of proof can be viewed in various ways, depending on the given perspective, context, and sociological context. In the laboratory, various mathematical and physical premises appropriate to this context are valid for the verification of truth claims. These premises are worked out in the course of interactions in this environment, i.e., among scientific colleagues, who have very definite ideas about what constitutes scientific proof. In this context, there is virtually no room for pure faith in the truth of something. Scientific proof is established in accordance with very definite principles (repeatability, comprehensibility, logic, etc.).

Religious scientists have to adhere to the established prerequisites for proof in order to gain recognition for their work and their results. In this context, they themselves would not accept any proofs on the part of fellow colleagues who did not proceed on the basis of the same methodology. Here, then, an interaction takes place that is based on certain conventions and agreements.

Religious premises of truth claims are developed in a completely different way. Religion does not rely on physically measurable, evaluable, and calculable ratiocinations. In the sphere of religion, faith constitutes the foundation of the religious determination of truth. In Christianity, Judaism, or Islam, faith is elucidated in holy scriptures that clearly lay down ethical and moral norms in the form of commandments and practical wisdom.

The religious person infers the existence of God on the basis of personal experiences, upbringing, and his or her immediate environment. Experience is all the proof that is required. There is no need for mathematically quantifiable empirical research.

The figure below expresses a visual perspective for understanding the difference between one-to-one communication and understanding on the meta-level.

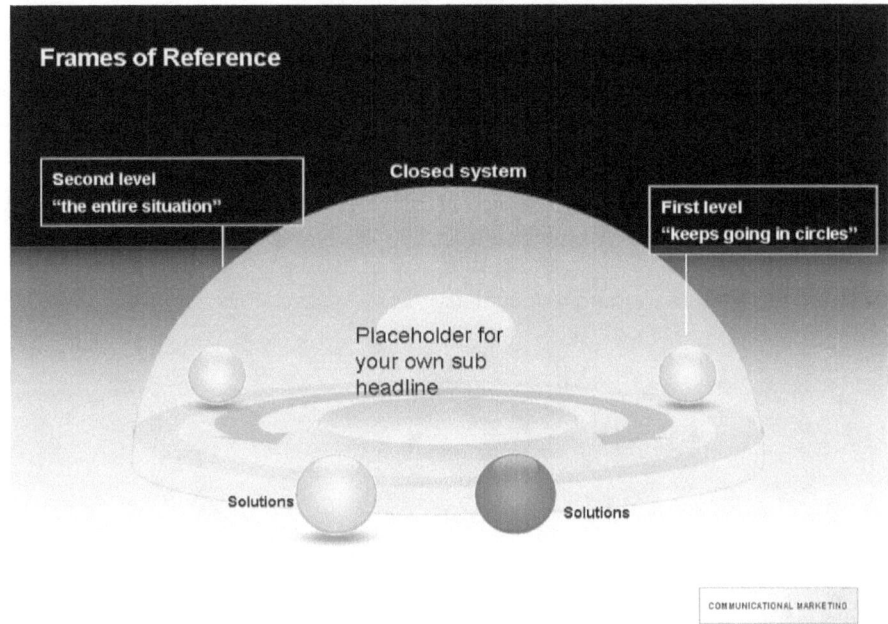

Here two definitions of proof have been presented whose basic premises are fundamentally at variance with each other. Who would want to claim which represents the sole truth for all people at all times?

Religious scientists have the ability to metacommunicate. This means the ability, in the course of interaction, to analyze themselves, their respective dialogue partners, and the context. Thus, no contradiction arises for them at all between the scientific theory of evolution and the religious account of creation. They can therefore think scientifically, on the one hand ,and at the same time accept the religious approach to truth without getting into a conflict.

Everyone has heard the remark, "We don't speak the same language." This is obviously not an observation about one's native language. What it is about is the different understanding each interlocutor has of the meaning of certain concepts. This indicates an awareness that intercommunicative tolerance can be attained by metacommunication.

In the example of the religious scientist, a problem is avoided by not looking for a solution at just one level. For no solutions are possible at this "first level." The attempt to find a solution at this level just leads to the creation of a real problem. Only the intellectual switch to the "second level" (metacommunication) puts the dialogue partners in a position to understand the situation as a whole. This means they have to stop to think about what they think and what is their opinion. They have to think about how they communicate. The only solution is to leave the actual scenario of communication and act like a third party who is listening to the conversation. Here, at this level, solutions are possible.

When you realize how your customers communicate and—this is decisive—how they see both you and themselves in the dialogue context, then their behavior will become easier to understand. Try it out! If metacommunication is successful, then the question of the individual causes of behavior, which are highly speculative anyway, becomes irrelevant.

Chapter 6
The Problem of Proof in the Social Sciences

Along with the natural sciences, philosophy, ethics and modern—particularly Western—theology, the sciences of behavior and communication also attempt by methodological means to solve, or get closer to solving, the central questions of human existence—in the present case, that of human behavior. The resulting practice of the isolated analysis of individual subproblems is certainly legitimate. This procedure is in full accordance with the logical principle that states "If you have a big problem, divide it up into a number of individual subproblems and construct a general concept from the resulting partial solutions." With the present-day level of knowledge, there is no other methodology available for the social and natural sciences.

Sir Karl R. Popper writes in his main work, *The Open Society and Its Enemies*:

> Social life is not only a test of strength between opposing groups. It is also behavior in a more or less resisting framework of institutions and traditions. And it leads, apart from conscious countermeasures, to many unforeseen reactions within this framework, some of which cannot be foreseen at all ... The main task of the social sciences consists, as I see it, in the attempt to analyze these reactions and anticipate them as far as possible.... One of the most primitive economic situations may serve as example in order to make clear the idea of the unintentional consequences of our actions: If somebody wants to buy a house urgently, one can assume most definitely that they don't wish to increase the market price of the house. But precisely the circumstance that they

31

turn up as a buyer on the market will have the tendency of increasing the market price.[3]

The natural sciences have an easier task of verifying their claims. Here, as a rule, new conclusions are drawn on the basis of partial results that have already been achieved and are then proven theoretically with the help of mathematics, statistics, group psychology, etc. Oskar Heinroth, a mentor of Konrad Lorenz, once said to his student, "What one thinks is mostly false, but what one knows is correct!"[4] This statement describes the typical genesis of perhaps every kind of human knowledge. One starts off by thinking that something is the case; then one compares it with one's store of individual experience; further data emerge, and then on the basis of agreement or disagreement a conclusion is drawn about the correctness or falseness of what one had thought in the first place.

Certain precisely defined suppositions (experimental conditions) form the foundation of every scientific experiment. These suppositions constitute a prerequisite for the success or the implementation of the measures taken. If, as in chemistry, there is in the end an "intense stink or explosion," the experiment can under certain circumstances be designated as successful, whereby the original hypothesis or assertion is proven.

Thus, the dilemma in the studies and observations of the social sciences lies in the verification procedures for their hypotheses.

In the study of human behavior, for example, quantifiability as applied as a standard instrument in physics becomes a problem. Scientific experiments and studies receive a certain degree of general validity if they can be repeated anytime with the same or similar results. The experimental setup, the theoretical model, or the underlying parameters of a biological experiment, for example, can be completely unrealistic and still receive the highest degree of recognition, all the way to a Nobel Prize, if they simply meet the requirement of being repeatable under the same premises. This raises questions about the tenability of the foundation of the scientific understanding of general validity and hence of "truth."

In the humanities and social sciences, it is hardly possible to set up experimental conditions. The legitimacy of drawing conclusions for human behavior from animal behavior is limited. Quantifiability, repeatability, and

---

[3]   Popper, Sir Karl R. *Die offene Gesellschaft und ihre Feinde* (" The Open Society and Its Enemies). Tübingen: J.C.B. Mohr, 1992.
[4]   Lorenz, Konrad. *Das sogenannte Böse* ("So-Called Evil"). 9th printing. dtv Sachbuch, 1981.

a resulting general valid synthesis in the form of a proof are in many cases impossible to attain.

Business psychology, which is the academic foundation of present-day marketing, bases its findings to some extent on empirical surveys. In innumerable experiments with test subjects, attempts have been made to determine the influence of advertising on human behavior in all kinds of situations. In order to obtain impartial results, the real motivation for the experiment is usually not told to the test subjects. If the respective underlying laboratory conditions are altered even slightly, or the conditions broadened, the ensuing results deviate from what previously had been empirically proven.

Let us take as an example the fantastic women and men portrayed in advertising. Less attractive persons are infrequently employed in advertising, apart from particularly unattractive models who radiate a certain originality. The long-running trend has been more in the direction of associating products with models who are beautiful, young, slim, modern, successful, dynamic, etc. And there is an apparently good (psychological) reason for this. Some psychological studies concerning the effect of attractive and less attractive persons on the judgment of the observer suggest that "good-looking" individuals radiate more likability, credibility, trustworthiness, and know-how. Advertising psychology therefore recommends portraying attractive persons in visual advertising material (newspaper ads, commercials, posters).

The assumption is that the positive impression created by the beautiful person becomes associated with the product portrayed alongside the model. In the 1980s, Forkan and Hawkins developed the "match-up hypothesis"[5] along these lines. Here the assumption of attraction by association is at least differentiated to the extent of maintaining that there should be some sort of objective connection between any given product and the "star" associated with it. Thus, the highest advertising success is supposed to be achieved if, for example, a well-known race driver promotes cars or a top model advertises lipsticks. Further studies (by Caballero and Pride[6], for example) went on to distinguish between products that are attractiveness-relevant and those that are not. According to these studies, it does not make any difference whether or not a particularly good-looking model is used for product categories, such as typing paper, computers, or umbrella stands. With respect to such products

---

[5]   Forkan, J. "Product Match-Up Key to Effective Star Presentations." *Advertising Age* 51 (6) (1980): 42.

[6]   Caballero, M.J. and Pride, W.M. "Selected Effects of Salesperson Sex and Attractiveness in Direct Mail Advertisements." *Journal of Marketing* 48 (1984): 94–100.

as cosmetics, cars, or fashion articles, on the other hand, people's readiness to buy is supposed to be heightened when the products are shown to be employed by particularly good-looking persons.

From a psychological point of view, these findings sound logical and plausible enough. But have you ever bought a product because of the model portrayed along with it? Do stars like Claudia Schiffer, Tom Selleck, Dennis Rodman, or Sam Waterston form the basis of your investment decisions? Does the sight of attractive or famous individuals mesmerize you to such an extent that you unthinkingly pull out your wallet?

An empirical study conducted in 1995 by Hans Mayer and Sonja Bundschuh at the University of Mannheim arrived at very interesting results on the "effects of the attractiveness of social models on product image and prospective buying behavior"—results that were contrary to the initial assumptions. The scientists confronted 160 test subjects with two products: a desk chair, which was defined as an attractiveness-irrelevant product; and sunglasses, the advertising effect of which was assumed to depend to a certain extent on the attractiveness of the person portrayed. In addition, three categories were specified in terms of which the test subjects were to detail their impression: elegance, value, and solidity of construction. The mean values tabulated in the study show that an attractive model does not necessarily bring about greater advertising success for an attractiveness-relevant product, and an unattractive model is not always a better complement for an attractiveness-irrelevant product. The scientists conclude their study by stating the following: "The sole categorization of products as attractiveness-relevant or attractiveness-irrelevant does not constitute a usable decision-making aid. Hence the truth value of the match-up hypothesis continues to remain doubtful."

As empirical studies seem to confirm, self-directed persons do not necessarily act in ways assumed by so much of "psychological logic." To prevent misunderstandings, I would like to point out that intrapsychic mechanisms as such are not being contradicted here in general. Particularly beautiful or sexually appealing people do constitute a stimulus, as has been shown by the above example. In order to be noticed at all, advertising should contain a certain entertainment aspect. What is being put into question, however, is the causal relationship between psychological methodology and the success of an advertisement. The magic word here is "suggestion." In psychology, "suggestion" is defined as "compulsive influencing with the circumvention of rational conviction." One has to let this definition sink in. When all is said and done, the advertising psychologist assumes that it is enough to have a top model pose next to his company's products in order for the "rational conviction of the consumer to be circumvented" by means of such visual suggestion.

A highly arbitrary conception of the human being seems to be at work here. This view of human beings has no basis in reality, at least with regard to consumers who lack a pathological disposition.

Part 1 Summary

In Part One, you became acquainted with the laws in operation whenever communication occurs. You now understand that it is impossible not to communicate. Hence the intent to avoid communication within an interaction is pointless.

An informational or content-related aspect and at least one relational aspect are essential characteristics of communication. The "healthier" an occurrence of communication is, the more content there is at the informational level. In conflictive or suggestive communication patterns, the relational level becomes decidedly more pronounced.

The course of an interaction can be symmetrical or complementary. Under certain circumstances, influence can be exerted on which of the interlocutors occupies the symmetrical or complementary position.

Corresponding to the fact that communication consists of an informational aspect and a relational aspect, digital and analogous elements can be identified. As a rule, the digital elements reinforce the informational aspect. At the relational level, communication takes place in the analogous mode.

In order to understand communication—i.e., any given communicational interaction—communication has to take place at the metalevel. Metacommunication makes it possible to gain a perspective from the outside, despite our own involvement in any given issue. If one understands communication as behavior that takes place within a referential system, then metacommunication means ascending to the next higher level. At this level, we no longer speak about something particular, a particular form of behavior, or a response; rather we observe *how* we talk *about* such things.

In Part Two, you shall learn the practical consequences of communicational laws. You shall see how you yourself are subject to these rules and how you can make use of them in order to avoid—or at least to analyze—conflicts.

Part Two

Confusion,
Paradoxical
Communication,

Subtle Influencing
The best and surest disguise is still the unvarnished truth.
That no one believes.

—Max Frisch

Chapter 7
Confusion Everywhere

The more complex and sophisticated the development of digital communication systems becomes, the greater the danger of errors and misunderstandings. Language with its manifold facets constitutes one of the most treacherous sources in this respect.

Upon being asked why the Mona Lisa smiles, an eight-year-old child replied: "One evening Mr. Lisa came home from work and asked Mona Lisa, 'What did you do today?' Mona Lisa smiled and said, 'Guess what? Leonardo came and painted my picture.'"[7]

"Is telephoning going to get more expensive?"

"Yes!"

"Is telephoning going to get cheaper?"

"Yes!"

"Huh?"

"The telephone company's new rate system is better than you think."

"Oh, how glad I am that I cannot stand spinach! Because if I liked it, then I would eat it—but I hate the stuff!"

Perhaps these examples have made you feel somewhat perplexed. This is typical reaction to communicational *confusions*.

Confusion can arise by one person's not understanding a certain situation or the behavior of another person. In this context, failing to understand does not mean the lack of the intellectual capacity to understand; it means, rather, the inability to harmonize an experience with one's own frame of reference.

Not infrequently, the reason for family conflicts lies in the emergence of confusion. If, for example, a family member is reproached by its (vital)

---

[7] Watzlawick, Paul. *Wie wirklich ist die Wirklichkeit?* ("How Real Is Reality?"). 17th edition. Munich: R. Piper & Co., 1992.

communication partners (e.g., a child by its parents) for its perception of reality and for the forms in which it defines itself, this could result in either a tendency to mistrust its own perception or a switch to a full counterattack.

A certain sense of uncertainty arises, which prompts the communication partner to insist on him or her starting to see things the right way. If the person told to conform doesn't comply, things can go so far that he or she gets accused of being crazy for having such "abnormal" opinions.

We are confronted daily with occurrences that don't seem to make sense right away. In fact, any number of forms of behavior elude every attempt at understanding—politics, for example. In confused situations, strong, self-confident individuals are inclined to do a reality check based on their frame of reference; if there is a total lack of conformity in a given situation, their means of coping with the confusion is rejection. Thus, for them confusing situations do not pose any real problem. Confusion amounts to nothing more than a minor difficulty.

Things look different in the case of a less strong, "unstable" person. If such a person is confronted with a confusing situation, he tends to search in a more and more defensive and vehement manner for new contexts of meaning and a more straightforward structure of reality. He gets the impression that everyone else has "got the picture" and that he alone is wandering around in a state of complete puzzlement. Here a real problem has indeed developed out of the communicational situation. In the worst-case scenario, an intensification of this behavior could go all the way from inner insecurity to schizophrenic behavior. In conflictive family relationships, it can be observed that one member is reproached by another for not feeling the way he or she ought to feel. The accused member ultimately feels guilty for not being able to exhibit the right kind of feeling.

At the workplace, this dilemma can be observed in a situation where a supervisor is totally convinced of the frequent assumption that a "properly managed" employee always has to seem happy, evenly balanced, and content. As a result, at the slightest sign of a bad mood on the part of an employee, this superior immediately thinks he recognizes a silent protest or even doubts about the superior's leadership qualities. Not infrequently, the superior reacts defensively with a counteraccusation denying the right of the employee to negative moods, saying something like: "After everything that the company has done for you and with the money that you earn, you ought to be happier and more content!"

In this way, even the slightest negative indication by an employee is interpreted as a sign of poor work morale and general negativity. It is clear that in the long run this will lead to severe problems.

Chapter 8
The Communicational Double Bind

The logical structure of our languages, the thought processes that are directly and fundamentally connected with them, as well as our perceptions in general, are based on the principle of contradiction. Since the contradictions of daily life do not automatically have to be pathological (this, at any rate, is the assumption here), in the event of contradictory directives everyone is at liberty to opt for one or the other. An illogical directive or command does not therefore have to be absolutely paradoxical. Despite the illogic, there is still the possibility of deciding for one of the alternatives.

With respect to the double bind, the situation is different. Here two mutually exclusive alternatives are presented. The one confronted with this situation also has to make a choice between alternatives; whatever choice is made in this case, however, will invariably turn out to be false.

Buy two luxurious evening dresses for your wife or girlfriend. The first time she wears one of them, ask her why she happened to select that one and if she doesn't like the other one! The double bind is perfect. (This will, of course, work equally well with men given two neckties.) Whenever these kinds of communication patterns become habitual in relationships, there are definitely going to be problems.

Persons who regularly get entangled in double binds cease to find solutions anymore. Their view of reality gets put completely in question. Psychoanalysis and psychiatry define schizophrenia superficially as an intrapsychic disorder: split personality, disordered thought processes, ego weakness, mental turmoil in primary processes, etc. The social environment of a person who has been diagnosed as schizophrenic can be incorporated in a therapeutic approach. But despite the inclusion of those involved (usually the family) in the "treatment," the issue is usually not raised that schizophrenia might be a product of these relationships themselves.

Here, however we shall be less concerned with the clinical picture of double binds and more with their consequences in completely normal intercommunications. We shall examine the conditions created for double binds by interpersonal communication.

1. Two or more communicants are involved in a relationship with one another that has a certain degree of meaning for at least one and perhaps more of the participants. Such situations exist in a sales talk between two old business acquaintances, in a family, between doctor and patient, between therapist and client, or in an interpersonal situation characterized by material dependence.

2. In the context of the relationship, something is communicated that a) contains a statement, and b) communicates something about the statement. This characteristic was already dealt with in the discussion of the essence of an item of communication in Axiom No. 2 (informational and relational levels).

3. A double bind—and this is what makes the phenomenon so confusing and so fascinating at the same time—is put together in such a way that the two statements (i.e., the statement itself and the communication about the statement) are incompatible with each other; each contradicts and negates the other.

An example: Advise your customer in view of the poor economic situation to save money but to buy your products nevertheless—since he or she will save money that way. On the one hand, the customer is told not to invest, but as soon as she does so she negates the second instruction of your message, namely to spend money at your establishment (if only in order to economize). If the customer starts thinking about investing with you, your other suggestion—i.e., that she save money—will stand in the way. However your customer twists and turns, she cannot follow your suggestion fully since each of the alternative actions contradicts the other. This should serve as a caution against advertising slogans that encourage customers to "save" on the one hand, and then animate them to buy a product on the one hand. This constellation can lead to the double-bind mechanisms described above and thus to practically insoluble confusion.

One cannot not react to a double bind, but on the other hand one cannot behave in an appropriate (unparadoxical) way toward it either, because the proposed course of action is paradoxical in itself.

A person caught in a double bind runs the risk of being chided by his counterpart for correctly perceiving the situation, as well as being called malicious or crazy should this person dare to claim that there is a substantial difference between his real perceptions and that which he is "supposed" to see.

Double binds are occasional and usually only temporary occurrences. As a rule, we manage to cope with them, if by no other way than by attempting to ignore them.

But double binds can become a chronic phenomenon and thus gradually turn into a habitual expectation. This, of course, applies primarily to children, since all children tend to draw the conclusion that their own experiences are the same as those of everyone else and must therefore have universal validity, as it were. Hence, advertising can indeed be dangerous for children if it becomes the basis for their perception of reality. Small children, for example, think that if they put their hands over their eyes, they have hidden themselves and cannot be seen by anyone. They draw the following conclusion: "If I can't see anything, then others can't see anything, either."

The effect of the double bind described above seems to turn the symptoms of schizophrenia into a specific structure of communication. Double binds are therefore not simply contradictory inducements to action, they are truly paradoxical ones. There is a fundamental difference between a contradictory directive on the one hand and a paradoxical directive (double bind) on the other. This difference is of great significance for the formulation of advertising messages, since the practical effects of these two types of directives are very different, as will be shown in the following section.

Experiments with the Double Bind

In various experiments in which an organism is exposed to a double-bind situation, the nature of the conflict becomes clear in the contradiction between the alternatives that are commanded on the one hand, and the ones that are actually forced upon the animal on the other. The behavioral effects of these experiments can range from indecision or erroneous decisions up to starvation (in animal experiments), as a result of the avoidance of further electrical shocks. In order for pathological symptoms to manifest themselves, however, the induced conflict has to first become paradoxical.

The reader is no doubt aware of the Pavlovian experiments with dogs. The above-described pathology can be observed in the famous Pavlovian experiments in which a dog is first taught the difference between a circle and an ellipse, whereupon the distinction is then made increasingly difficult and finally impossible to discern. The ellipse is changed step by step in such a manner that it increasingly approaches a circular form—i.e., so that it can be hardly recognized as an ellipse anymore. The criteria of the double bind are very clearly implemented in this animal experiment.

The Double Bind

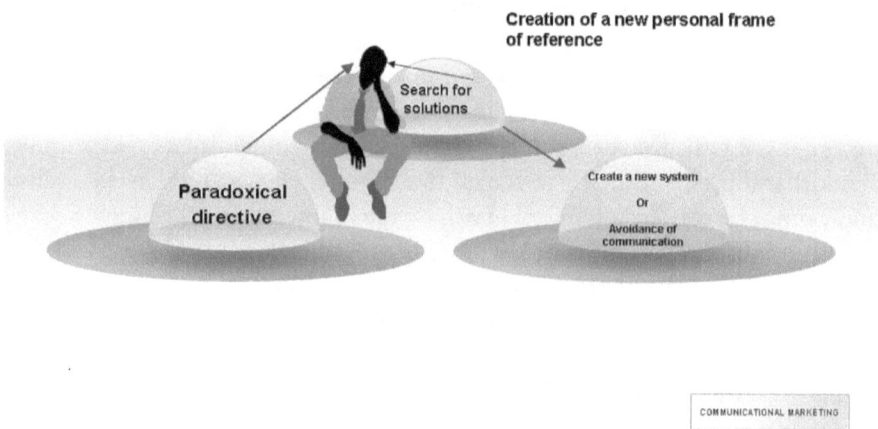

The conductor of the experiment first forces upon the laboratory animal the life-and-death necessity of correctly distinguishing between a circle and an ellipse. Within this restricted framework, the experimenter then renders the distinction impossible for the animal to make. The dog is forced into a world in which its survival depends on the compliance with a law—having to distinguish between a circle and an ellipse in order to get food. With the increasing conformity between the circle and the ellipse the law itself is abrogated; it excludes itself, as it were, whereupon the paradox is completed.

At this stage of the experiment, experimenters observed how the laboratory animal started to show typical behavioral disorders: it sank into a coma or even became extremely aggressive and ill-tempered. In addition, it exhibited all the physical symptoms of great anxiety.

To summarize: the most essential difference between a merely contradictory command and a paradoxical command consists in the fact that, in the former case, one has to choose one alternative, thereby losing the other. In the case of the contradictory command, therefore, a choice remains logically possible. The paradoxical command, on the other hand, makes the choice itself impossible; neither the one alternative nor the other is really a valid option.

In the following, it shall be assumed that the basic definition of the double bind and its specific features have become clear. The consequences of the double-bind mechanism for the formulation of advertising messages are discussed in the next section. Let us now consider the practical consequences.

The Double Bind in Advertising Messages

The effects of a double bind on human behavior are of the greatest interest for entrepreneurial marketing and for the understanding of the communicational processes connected with it. Frequently, double binds get built into advertising or even into the overall image of companies, presumably willy-nilly and without awareness of the communicational consequences. Because of the strong effect of the double-bind mechanism, however, after a few general remarks the attempt will be made in the first example below to utilize the double bind within an advertising message.

In a relationship, each individual communication reduces the number of the next possible communications—for everything communicated by a transmitter, in whatever form, ultimately deprives the recipients of the possibility of being able to formulate just this communication themselves. As a rule, prior to a buying decision by the customer there are only a few short interactions. After a certain period of lack of interest, the customer will switch off and not enter into any further interactions. This reduces the number of next possible persuasive communications even further.

In the case of double binds, this increasing behavioral restriction is particularly drastic, and only a very few responses are possible. Some of the reactions to double binds that are most important for entrepreneurial communication shall be set forth in the following.

In view of the untenable absurdity of every double-bind situation, the person affected can be inclined to think that she must have overlooked significant clues or indications. It can be suspected that these clues are a) to be found in the situation, or b) to have been provided by the other persons involved.

The latter possibility will probably just amplify the uncertainty of the person affected, for it will create the impression that the others view the situation as completely natural and intelligible. The suspicion will then arise that meaningful clues are being deliberately withheld. Think back on a situation in which you were confronted with something (in a group) that you simply could not comprehend in the slightest. Your first reaction was probably to look around and check the reactions of the others. If they showed no signs of bewilderment, you quite likely started to have doubts about yourself.

There are people, however, who are true artists in hiding their own lack of understanding. Even if they have understood absolutely nothing—at a lecture, for example—they don't reveal a single telltale sign. Some listeners even manage to put on such convincing expressions of competence that they create the impression of having understood everything. The apparent know-it-all will quickly find himself or herself in an awkward predicament, however, if are addressed either by the speaker, who feels understood and confirmed by the affirmatively nodding listener, or by another listener who is at a total loss and in desperation asks the would-be know-it-all to explain something. But now let us return to the double bind.

As a consequence of the uncertainty of the situation, the person caught in a double bind will look for other solutions, which might well be entirely eccentric. The result of this search for a new frame of reference could then become her new truth.

And precisely this behavioral model prompted the author to formulate the strategy of intercommunicative double-bind (SID) logic in advertising.

The SID works as follows. First, a clear objective is stated with an advertising message—for example, "The least expensive car in the world." A formulated advertising objective can become truth if it serves as an escape from a double bind. Here the double bind has the function of inducing the person being addressed to consciously search for new realities, i.e., solutions. If the advertising objective itself becomes the solution, you have won the game. Your advertising claim then becomes the "truth" in the eyes of the perceiver.

A double bind incorporated into an advertising message will receive the highest degree of attention if it unites all the characteristics of the paradox (and this is the prerequisite, for otherwise the double bind loses its functional foundations), while at the same time offering a solution at another level—a solution that can be grasped as the "truth."

The advertising text in the next illustration constitutes a typical example of a paradoxical inducement: On the one hand, the customer is advised not to spend any money. On the other hand, he is supposed to treat himself to the car. This inducement is paradoxical and excludes complete compliance with it. Without the illustration—which constitutes a solution as an outsider factor, so to speak—the advertisement would be a fatal mistake from a communicational point of view, as was pointed out in the previous section. The creation of double binds should be avoided in the context of advertising claims! In the search for a solution for the paradox, the illustration, which is directly connected with the brand name JAPANO CAR, comes into play.

Looking at the advertisement will necessitate that the viewer find clues. She will feel pressured to extend the vain search for a meaning to improbable and unrelated phenomena.

Instead of embarking on an endless search for hidden meanings in the text, (which, to repeat, attempts to induce a paradoxical act) the viewer will in this case only be willing to pay attention to the most superficial aspects. He will therefore reject a priori the possibility that messages can be differentiated at different levels of reality. Through the use of the word *save,* the graphic implies that the product is inexpensive. That makes the Japano car an inexpensive automobile.

It makes sense that the second, real advertising claim in the form of the graphic becomes understood and internalized as the "truth"; it is understandable in itself. At least the characteristic "inexpensive" can be positioned effectively for the brand Japano car. Empirical studies are intended to demonstrate further aspects of the SID strategy.

The use of double binds in the formulation of advertising messages is risky, for a further possible reaction to the double-bind phenomenon consists in the attempt to withdraw from the relationship in question—as far as the impossibility of not communicating permits. And exactly this has become the most frequent reaction to bad advertising—it gets switched off.

Communication cannot be avoided, as even physical withdrawal communicates a statement of its own—for example: "This advertisement is getting on my nerves!" Withdrawal from a relationship can be accomplished largely by physical self-isolation. Where this isolation is not possible to the desired extent, withdrawal can be accomplished by blocking reception of the communication.

Double binds get problematic if they become the rule in communication and if, because of this situation, the person affected tries to avoid communication altogether. Persons who isolate themselves in this way seem to other people to be withdrawn, inaccessible, or even autistic. In an extreme case, the double-bind victim will even describe himself or herself as depressive and, caught in a double bind, will under no circumstances even consider fighting against this depression, which functions as a home remedy for getting out of a double bind.

A therapist who looks for the psychological causes of a depression runs the risk of reinforcing the depressive symptom precisely by arduously and intensively probing into the psyche of the "patient," namely by reinforcing the double bind underlying the depression even more by suggestive interventions. This effect has the consequence that the victim hangs on even more tightly to his remedy for the confusion resulting from the double bind: "I want to be depressive because I have to be in order to cope with all the confusion." Company executives should be aware of this! The more vehement the attempt to combat this self-regulating mechanism, the more the effect is reinforced.

Practically the same result—i.e., the attempt to flee from double binds—can be achieved by hyperactive or aggressive, hysterical behavior intense and continual enough to practically drown out all communicative input from the environment.

Everybody is familiar with similar situations, perhaps not so dramatic but revealing nonetheless: talk shows, for example, or the turbulent, highly emotional debates of worked-up politicians who constantly interrupt each other and refuse to stick to the subject. Because of all the chaos, no one can any longer follow the arguments of the other side. This obviously paradoxical behavior can also be interpreted as an attempt to avoid communicating.

Whoever receives behavioral directives (from people with whom they are involved or upon whom they are materially dependent) that simultaneously require and forbid certain forms of behavior are put in a paradoxical situation in which they can only comply with what is demanded from them by not complying. The basic message in this paradox is: "Don't do what I want you to do, do what I tell you to do." Here are some examples.

- Parents expect their son to have respect for law and order but at the same time to act in a more dynamic and audacious manner.
- Company executives insist on dynamic, successful, sales-oriented, and hard-nosed sales personnel. However, in their dealings with customers, the same sales personnel are expected to put on a highly respectable and dignified show.
- Parents place great value on "champion children" such that it sometimes sees as though almost any means to this end will do. On the other hand, they insist on humaneness, fairness, cooperation, and honesty from their child at all times.
- A mother warns her daughter at a very early age about the ugliness and dangers of sexuality but at the same time makes it unmistakably clear that a woman is supposed to look alluring in order to be desired and courted by men.

As these examples show, the double bind is anything but a purely clinical, pathological phenomenon. Every single day, we run the risk of getting entangled in double binds ourselves or of putting others in such a situation. The most frequent reaction seems to be withdrawal from communication. This makes the double bind such a fatal mistake in advertising.

An even more frequent paradox is described in the following chapter. This paradox is probably the most widespread way of putting consumers in a state of confusion.

Chapter 9

The "Be Spontaneous!" Paradox

This paradox involves the particularly odd and confusing predicament that arises when one party demands a specific, spontaneous form of behavior from the other.

What makes the demand "Be spontaneous!" paradoxical? To clarify the nature of this paradox, think what the demand "Be spontaneous!" really means: being told to do something without first having to be told to do so. However, now it is impossible to comply with this (perhaps even well-meant) bidding; the person asked or told cannot act spontaneously because this has already been demanded of them.

Spontaneity means doing something without having been prompted by others to do it. If the action of the person prompted is preceded by a prompt, then whatever else her reaction may be (original, humorous, peculiar), it can no longer be spontaneous. That is what makes the call for spontaneity paradoxical.

Depending on the strength of the underlying need, these so-called "Be spontaneous!" paradoxes can range from harmless disputes up to the most tragic complications. One of the many curiosities of human communication is the impossibility of inducing another person to spontaneously fulfill a wish or satisfy a need. Spontaneity that is prompted leads rather to the paradoxical situation that the prompt itself makes its fulfillment impossible.

This communication pattern can frequently be observed in the daily interaction between sales managers and their sales representatives. Sales representatives are supposed to make sales. This is the justification for their existence. For many companies it is a secondary issue how the sales volume is achieved. What counts is the bottom line. On the other hand, sales representatives are always expected to put on a respectable appearance and not let it be noticed that they have to sell. They are supposed to be

50

dynamic and at the same time radiate an aura of calm. They are not supposed to lose any customers, but they shouldn't let it show that their company needs customers. Here the unenviable employees are not only involved in a double bind, they are also confronted with the requirement of being nice and friendly. Being nice and friendly, however, are characteristics of spontaneous emotional impulses. If I ask you on the spot not only to be friendly but also to feel good about it, this won't be easy for you. You can meet a pleasant person and spontaneously react in a friendly way, but you usually can't do it as a knee-jerk response to a demand.

The "Be spontaneous!" mechanism also works to the disadvantage of the person who sets it in motion. This problem can be illustrated by the following example: A wife hints to her husband to bring her flowers or little presents once in a while, the way the husband of her friend always does. Since she has probably longed for this small token of love for a long time, her wish is thoroughly understandable. What is less obvious is the fact that, in this way, she herself has unfortunately destroyed the possibility of having her longing for this token of love fulfilled. If her husband ignores her wish, she will continue to feel less loved; however, if he acts on her prompting, then she will be dissatisfied nevertheless, for he didn't give her the flowers spontaneously on his own initiative but only because she asked for this gesture.

Something quite similar can happen to parents who, for example, consider their son to be too soft and compliant and therefore try to hammer into him some variation of: "Don't be such a softy!" Here again only two results are possible, both of which are unsatisfactory: In the first case, the boy remains passive. The parents will be dissatisfied since he doesn't comply with their wish for him to show a little more backbone. In the second case, he changes his behavior in the desired way. But his parents will nevertheless be dissatisfied in this case as well because he is behaving "correctly" for the wrong reason, namely out of excessive compliance.

Thus, all those involved in this kind of interpersonal dilemma are more or less victims, but the person who probably bears the most responsibility in any given case is the one who demanded spontaneity in the first place.

The "Be Spontaneous!" Trap in Marketing

The "Be spontaneous!" paradox turns up frequently in advertising. Here it occurs frequently in its "inverted" form as well.

Some examples from well-known TV and radio advertisements might help to clarify the point.

Look forward to our new spring collection!

Let yourself be enchanted by the flair..

Be our guest and enjoy yourself.
Put yourself in the position of a rich man.
Become happier by using our product.
You are always welcome! (Inversion)

The illustration shows a special variant of the "Be spontaneous!" paradox—i.e., its *inversion*.

The sense of the statement "You are always welcome!,"—i.e., an invitation, is contradicted by the form in which this statement is communicated. A warmly and sincerely meant invitation has real meaning only if it is extended on an individual and spontaneous basis. However, this is contradicted by the doubt that arises in the mind of those addressed about whether they really are personally welcome. Such *advertising* can be found in business travel guides, for example. Now by virtue of the characteristic "advertisement," which per se is directed to entire groups, such an invitation can never be an individual one. To the contrary, earnestly meant personal invitations require a correspondingly personal form of address.

In this example, which I have called an "inversion" of the paradox, the paradox lies not in the *demand* for spontaneous behavior, but rather in the wholesale *offer* of pseudospontaneous hospitality. Recall the commercials on CNN done by a number of big hotel chains and club complexes: "You're always welcome!"

The "Be Spontaneous!" Paradox of a Bank

A clear-cut example of this paradox is provided by an expensive advertising campaign of the Deutsche Bank.

Deutsche's campaign depicts emotionally evocative scenes in television commercials and print advertisements, and on big posters put up in branch offices. The premise is characterized by events and life situations that awaken associations, such as "the beginning," "motivation," "success." These are all very positive emotions that are presented in impressive and plausible scenes. Thus, in television commercials, for example, in suspense-building slow-motion sequences, the viewer is made to feel he is watching footage of the takeoff of the first airplane, behind which a joyful technician is running and jumping into the air with excitement. In another, shorter sequence, the viewer sees a young gymnast working on a balance beam. The exercise is turning out well and is being watched approvingly by the coach or father, who has an extremely proud and deeply moved expression on his face. Another episode movingly depicts a young man making a marriage proposal to his female companion and tenderly putting an engagement ring on her finger. Of course, this story also concludes with a happy ending—in front of the church, with the couple dressed in conventional wedding attire, savoring the applause of the well-wishing congregation.

Up to this point, these thoroughly positive scenes are very realistically depicted. They awaken positive thoughts and memories on the part of viewers of experiences in which they themselves were perhaps equally successful or had an equally positive experience. But then comes the concluding slogan, which contains the motto of the advertising campaign: "Everything starts with trust. Deutsche Bank."

Unfortunately, this is another treacherous "Be spontaneous!" paradox that ruins the effect of the entire commercial, which otherwise is so effectively laid out. The reason is this: trust is a feeling, a disposition. Trust is a relationship that doesn't simply come about because it is asked for. But in this example that is exactly what the bank is trying to do. This is a completely typical and thoroughly telling example of the main thesis of this book, which puts in question the basic approach of advertising strategies based on psychological assumptions. Classical advertising strategists may be quite right from a psychological point of view when they assume that building trust between supplier and customer should constitute one of the primary objectives of marketing. (This will be confirmed in the last part of this book.) But due to its very nature, trust can by no means be gained by demanding it or asking for it—just as little as love, or affection, or the desire for something.

"Trust us!" contains the enjoinment to be spontaneous. But trust is the product of an individualized process that cannot be forced. The process of building trust has to come about by itself—spontaneously—if it is going to be genuine. Precisely the example of the "Trust us!" paradox clearly shows how essential the communicational aspect is in advertising messages.

Trust is explicitly demanded just as frequently in interpersonal relationships, which leads to the same kind of problems here as well; "You'll have to trust me ... if I am going to help you, if you really love me ..." The not-infrequent reply, "Okay, okay, I trust you," hardly constitutes a satisfactory compliance with this urging.

Trust is a theme that crops up repeatedly in advertising, such as that by insurance companies, banks, capital goods, and so forth. Illuminating in this connection are its origin, emergence, and development. Among infants an instinctive, primal trust can be observed, which apparently extends to all the people in their environment. The infant has not yet learned to distinguish whom or what could constitute a danger. The infant accepts everybody and does not yet show any signs of antipathy toward unfamiliar persons. It is not until later, at the small-child stage, that demonstrable signs of mistrust emerge. In some children, this mistrust of unknown persons, a phenomenon that is usually referred to as being "scared of strangers," can appear very suddenly. In the next phase, which is frequently connected with starting kindergarten or elementary school, the child begins to differentiate. Social behavior now becomes characterized by the fact that all persons must first demonstrate their deservingness of trust.

These characteristics of trust, which are clearly morally and culturally conditioned, have the consequence that trust appears to be an emotional product of various, highly individual processes. Hence trust cannot be demanded, as the Deutsche Bank attempted to do, or as can be seen in personal relationships.

However, the upshot of the publicity campaign of the Deutsche Bank was not just the emergence of the above-described paradox. Analyzing the message in terms of informational and relational levels in communication, identifies further concepts of interest. The digital message communicated by oral and written speech is "Everything starts with trust!" This factual statement could, no doubt, form the basis of an interesting philosophical discussion on the concept of trust. This statement doesn't necessarily have to correspond to an all-embracing truth. But it could reflect the truth of one's own worldview. It is clear to everyone, however, that the disinterested proclamation of theses for philosophical discussion is hardly a motivating factor for a major international bank—least of all in a television commercial. Therefore, behind the purely informational aspect—and this would hardly be denied by the advertising strategists in this campaign—there must be a further statement that "asks" for trust. Thus, the desired *relational* effect contains the following exhortation: "Trust us!" or "You can trust us!."

Since the relational aspect, which has been explained in detail above, characterizes paradoxes as well, it inevitably triggers the mechanisms of the double bind—with fatal consequences. As we have seen, in paradoxical situations a person tends to look for solutions, for some kind of ordering principle. However, solutions are not going to be found in the paradox itself. Therefore, in this case people will turn away because they cannot square their frame of reference or worldview (here their view of what trust is) with the demand for trust.

The situation has even more dramatic consequences for the advertising message if the recipient starts to build up defense mechanisms by reading other things into it. "What? They want my trust? They think they deserve it? They'll have to prove that first. And why do they insist so much on having my trust anyway? Obviously they need it so badly because they cannot be trusted in the first place."

If these exemplary associations at the relational level seem too far-fetched, recall the example of the interpersonal relationship: if trust is suddenly demanded by one partner, this circumstance alone often triggers mistrust. A really good and healthy relationship doesn't require constant declarations of trust. Trust is simply there and constitutes a foundation that has developed out of experiences with the other person. Only in conflict situations does it become an issue.

Paradoxes are universal and clearly do their mischief in all possible varieties of human relationships. In communication they have a lasting influence on the way human beings view reality. The semantic and communicational analysis of such concepts as trust, consistency, demonstrability, justice, normality, power, love, and health shows that these concepts often have a fatal tendency to generate paradoxes in advertising messages.

The following illustration introduces the Communicational Pyramid of Interactive Paradoxicality, otherwise known as the CIP Pyramid. This pyramid shows the virtually unstoppable momentum of the interactive path of a double-binding "Be spontaneous!" paradox.

The Communicational Pyramid

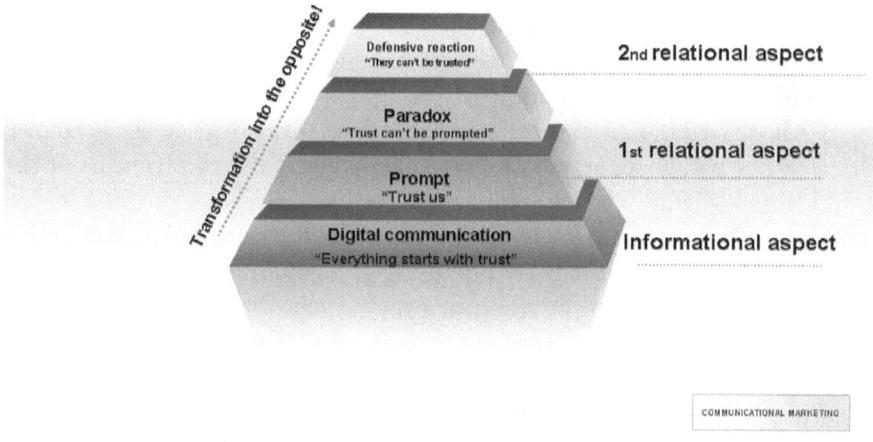

The mechanisms of the "Be spontaneous" paradox turn the digital message into its opposite: the defense mechanisms of the receiver turn the message against the sender. The demand for spontaneous trust generates mistrust; credibility turns into doubt; and confidence could, in this model, turn into anxiety.

Chapter 10

Paradoxes, Power, and Truth

Power produces its own particular paradoxes and double binds. This is clearly apparent in international political relations. In an interesting study, Peter Schmidt examined the relationship between the United States and Japan in the mid-1960s.[8] At the time, Japan lived under the shadow of U.S. economic might.

The communication between the two nations was clearly to the advantage of the United States. Americans were well aware of their ubiquitous economic power, which they demonstrated at every opportunity that presented itself. Compared to the United States, Japan was still a scarcely relevant factor on the world market.

"Power" writes Schmidt, "is evil; I renounce it, not entirely, but as far as possible. A friend protects me. He is powerful ... and that is bad.... I hate and despise him for it.... And yet I must give him my hand. I am powerless because I strive to be good.... My bad friend has power over me. I condemn what he does as a person with power, and yet I tremble at the thought that he could stumble. For if my protector tumbles, as befits those who are bad, then I too shall fall, the good person..."

"If my protector tumbles," Schmidt wrote, "I too shall fall." Power means dominance. The power component exhibits communicational relevance whenever a company, for example, has become so big (powerful) that it is "feared" by its own customers. Relationships of dependence develop between producers and distributors as well; the latter are often so dependent on the success of a manufacturer's products that they would inevitably fail if the source of their success, namely, the producer, were to dry up.

---

[8]   Schmidt, Peter. "Der japanische Hamlet" ("The Japanese Hamlet"). *Der Monat* 18 (August, 1966): 7.

Some big companies tend to demonstrate their power by putting on (psychologically sophisticated) "gala events." From a communicational point of view, this is self-glorifying and dangerous. Seen against its historical background, power always has an ominous quality about it. Companies run a high risk of demonstrating their power in advertising statements as well. To a certain extent the portrayal of company successes, record turnovers, and generous public gestures makes good sense. This provides assurance to customers that they are in good hands with a strong company that will be around a long time. The demonstration of a certain strength, liquidity, credit standing, and initiative is a good thing.

However, a demonstration of *power* will quickly cause the company to be looked upon as a dubious, threatening constellation. If the company is ever exposed as being overpowerful, overbearing, or even "obsessed with power," as some banks have increasingly been perceived recently, it is extremely difficult, if not impossible, to shed this image. Even large press conferences are then of little help—press conferences in which an admission of power is made but at the same time relativized both with the statement that this power is, of course, put only to positive use and with the request that customers have understanding and appreciation for the company's noblest of motives.

Lord Acton once wrote in an aphorism, "Power tends to corrupt the powerful." This thesis is an enlightening one. Less apparent is the fact that the conclusion that can be drawn from this—i.e., that power (seen here as the evil) is something to be avoided to the greatest extent possible—can lead to strange, paradoxical results. Where power clearly does exist—be it based on capital, social position, political connections, or whatever—then the denial of its existence means a fundamental disenfranchisement of those on the receiving end.

In company practice today, the attempt is again being made to cultivate a completely power- and pressure-free style of dealing with employees and customers, as well as suppliers. No mention is made of power in "total quality management," despite the fact that it is the completely dominant factor here and that adherence to "quality" denotes a degree of capability and thus power. However, real pathologies can be generated by existing power structures that are denied to exist.

Jean-Jacques Rousseau could be interpreted as defining a society that corrupts all the people who live in it. A basic idea of Rousseau's could be summarized in the following thesis: The human being is by nature good; it is society with its materialistic, utilitarian structures that leads human beings down the road to ruin. Modern companies in particular seem to be dedicated to the illusion that all their employees without exception are naturally motivated, willing to work, and good at heart. These characteristics (which probably are just dormant for the time being) could easily be reactivated again with a few motivational programs and methods employing psychological suggestion. Unfortunately, managers who adhere to this conception of the human being have still provided no explanation for the following question: how could this mass of innately good, motivated, and loyal employees ever turn against the company? Nor are proponents of such idealized conceptions of human nature able to explain how all these innately good human beings could be responsible for such problems as totalitarian oppression, suicide, divorces, crime, or child abuse.

Already in 1945, Karl Popper stated the following in his work *The Open Society and Its Enemies*: "The paradise of the happy, primitive society has been lost for all those who have eaten from the tree of knowledge."[9] Wherever power exists, in whatever form or over whatever subjects, the more emphatically it is denied by those with the power, the more threatening it becomes for those subject to its structures.

In marketing, demonstrations of power are completely out of place. Whoever strives for an image of competence, trust, or credibility by emphasizing their power is, from a communicational point of view, barking up the wrong tree. Power felt in relationships is readily amplified by those affected with negative associations, such as domineering behavior, submission, control, pressuring, exploitation, or manipulation.

Apart from the question of the social and entrepreneurial relationships to power just described, power at the interpersonal level becomes relevant to communication science whenever it manifests itself in a paradoxical form.

In company personnel policy, the attempt is also made to avoid all possible indications of power. According to a widely held view, one of the main premises of "modern leadership culture" is to deny existing power structures over against employees.

Many executives don't seem to be aware of the paradoxical situation into which they put subordinates with remarks like "Let's be friends"; "You can always trust me"; "I am always there for you." The attempt to deny existing power structures over against subordinates may at first glance seem very humane and noble, but the attempt leads to extremely curious results nonetheless.

One of the main tasks of the executive consists in motivating employees. By their own efforts, apparently, sales representatives couldn't accomplish this, for if they could then the function of the sales manager would be pointless.

---

[9]   Popper, Sir Karl R. *Die offene Gesellschaft und ihre Feinde* (" The Open Society and Its Enemies). Tübingen: J.C.B. Mohr, 1992.

The definition of the "motivated sales representative" is solely the product of the executive's view of reality—i.e., the idea of a motivated sales representative that the executive has in his or her mind. It goes without saying that this view is not "friendly" or even "neutral" but is subject to the expectations and goals of the executive in question.

Everybody knows best what reality means for them. And in our present context, "real" is behavior that can be squared with existing social norms and the objectives of the company. Everything that departs from this normative framework or raises doubts about it, let alone putting it radically in question, is labeled "abnormal" or even "subversive." One of the essential characteristics of this framework is the norm of spontaneous compliance. Hence, this characteristic is a norm of motivation models as well. A common denominator of a number of psychological methods can be expressed as follows: As far as possible, employees should learn on their own how to get control over their lives, find "meaning," and thus move on to achieve top performances. They should have "good morale," and they should love, if not their superiors, then at least their work and their company.

This normative description contains the requirement of spontaneously correct behavior. And until they start exhibiting this behavior, employees are in need of motivational support. Since assistance cannot be forced upon the employees, the only remaining avenue is that of *paradoxical influencing*.

Thus, it seems right in principle not to force anyone to attend sales meetings, for example. But failure to attend these meetings—where not infrequently the individual sales representatives attempt to outshine each other with their respective performance records—is sufficient proof for the boss or the superior that the absentees are unable—without assistance—to understand what is in their own best interests and then to act accordingly (i.e., go to the meetings). Therefore the executive must make the decision for them. Usually, this is handled in the following manner: The offenders are taken aside in a friendly manner and assured once again that attendance at these meetings is not compulsory. Then they are questioned closely about why they don't of their own accord want to let themselves be motivated.

The widespread assumption of the equality of all those involved (employees, executives, management) is absurd—if for no other reason than that every form of help presupposes a power structure between helper and helped. The assumption of equality has curious consequences as well, such as even greater insecurity, anxiety, and distancing from the supervising executive and the company. Instead of the desired identification effect, exactly the opposite is accomplished.

To deny power is to deny reality. Subordinate employees will keep on playing along with the "power-denial game" since they don't have to power to actively put an end to it. Interestingly enough, it is the particularly power-oriented supervisors who most frequently deny or at least keep on relativizing the reality of their power over their subordinates. But exactly this transparent suggestion of an apparently power-free relationship contains a schizophrenic denial of existing aspects of reality. Under such conditions, no conversation, no remark, no interaction, not even a gesture between a power-denying supervisor and ordinary employees can take place in a healthy and normal manner. The power-denying superior continually puts his "subordinate" in an unstable, insecure, and hence overly stressful situation. This can produce deep resentment, even hatred.

Where due to hierarchical structures or varying levels of know-how power structures objectively exist but are denied, there is not only insecurity but also a further problem for the recipient of those well-intentioned denials. By continually insisting that there is no overall power structure, exactly the opposite is signaled. In relationships where no power structures dominate, friendship predominates. But the general consensus is that friendship requires a certain degree of reciprocity. By insisting that no power structure exists, a person communicates their desire for friendship. On the one hand, this desire contains the offer "Let me be your friend!"; on the other hand, however, this wish also contains the demand "Accept me as your friend!"

This brings us right back to the classical "Be spontaneous!" paradox. A feeling of friendship always presupposes spontaneity; it cannot be simply demanded. The person confronted with the demand is maneuvered into a paradoxical situation. What happens? The mechanisms of the CIP Pyramid create the opposite of friendship—rejection, antipathy, enmity, or even hatred—out of the demand for it.

The superior who denies her power to a subordinate will not glean any real acknowledgment or satisfaction from this situation either. For if the subordinate gives in to the demand and does indeed behave in a friendly manner, the supervisor will have to assume that the employee is behaving that way only because of having been prompted to do so and is therefore not displaying genuinely friendly feelings toward the superior. The dissatisfaction of the superior is then deepened by the awareness that the subordinate is also indirectly contradicting her by understanding his own pseudospontaneous behavior as pure submission to the existing power structure.

The dangers connected with both the demonstration and the denial of power structures have no doubt become evident from the above. In all situations where power structures exist—whether between employees, between a company and a customer, or in private relationships—a diagnosis of the communicative interactions connected with the paradoxes of the power would therefore seem to be imperative.

Closer scientific observation of the effects of paradoxes on human behavior is a more recent branch of behavioral research. Present-day knowledge suggests that communication patterns excessively characterized by paradoxes can be regulated by means of a *counterparadox*.

Intuition, acting, and making decisions on the basis of common sense, as well as the creation of visions—all of these constitute accepted avenues of approach in modern management. Particularly in scientific circles, however, a certain suspicion of irrationality, fortuity, lack of scientific objectivity, or even esotericism still attaches to these kinds of interpretation of reality. And in most textbooks on marketing, as well as in the technical literature on economics, a view of reality based on common sense plays a subordinate role at best. If it is a question of intercommunication, however, and ultimately that is what marketing is all about, then we cannot avoid considering the communicational aspects of human behavior—with the result that behavior suddenly starts to become much more intelligible, logical, and plausible.

As we have seen, considerable confusion can arise from certain communication patterns. The next chapter shows that, in addition to the confusing and disturbing aspects, positive effects can also emerge from this confusion.

Chapter 11
Advantages of Confusion

In the light of the foregoing discussion, it would seem that all the confusions arising from paradoxes and their effects on human behavior are indicative of mechanisms that are hardly what we would call positive. Particularly in stable and enduring structures, such as those in companies, marriages, and other interpersonal relationships, paradoxes and the confusions arising from them seem to provide ideal incendiary material for misunderstandings and conflicts.

However, this is not altogether the case; confused situations can trigger certain regulatory mechanisms. And, as we shall see, in the context of the communication these mechanisms are of vital significance.

Imagine the following situation: You enter a room. Shortly thereafter, all the persons present break out in loud, resounding laughter. Some avert their glances in embarrassment. Others howl with laughter, slapping their thighs and gasping for breath. For you this behavior of your illustrious contemporaries is extremely confusing. For either the wildly enthusiastic spectators see something completely different in the situation than you see, or they are in possession of information of which you are completely unaware.

Your immediate response will probably be to look for plausible clues to the behavior of the other persons. Perhaps you will look around to see whether anyone near you is making faces. Or you might check your clothing and your face to see if you can find anything there that the others could find so amusing.

It wouldn't be difficult for students to cause their teacher a great deal of embarrassment by staring spellbound at a previously agreed-upon point of his or her body. It wouldn't take very long before the teacher either asked what the matter was or left the classroom in embarrassment to examine himself or herself for telltale signs.

Clearly, the state of confusion in which a person finds himself quickly leads, after a short paralysis or blackout, to a search for pointers (solutions) to the possible clarification of the uncertainties. It is hoped that these solutions will remove the discomfort and the apprehensiveness generated by the confusion.

Some typical forms of behavior follow from this: If the search for solutions remains unsuccessful, it is extended to all possible (and impossible) points of reference. Factors or reference points that under normal circumstances would never be taken into consideration suddenly receive the highest degree of attention. They constitute the ray of hope for the confused person. Even the most firmly held principles are suddenly jettisoned if doing so holds out any kind of promise of a solution to the situation. The most insignificant and out-of-the-way connections are now included for consideration.

A further form of behavior in confused situations is a particularly strong tendency to grab onto the first concrete explanation thought to be discerned in the fog of confusion. This was precisely the case in the example of the advertisement in which confusion was created in order to channel the viewer into an overarching frame of reference.

Let us now have a look at this form of behavior in which the person in question clings to the first reference points that offer themselves. The hypnotherapist Dr. Milton Erickson developed this behavior into a therapeutic approach he terms the "confusion technique." He discovered this approach by accident one day during an incident he described as follows.

"On a stormy day as I was struggling against the wind at a street corner, a man came around the corner quickly and in his haste bumped into me hard. Before he could recover from the shock and say something, I made a show of looking at my watch as if he had asked me the time. Then I said politely, 'It is exactly ten minutes to two,' although it was nearly four o'clock, and then I proceeded on my way. Several houses further on I turned round and saw that he was still looking after me, apparently still confused and disconcerted by my remark."[10]

In such perplexing situations, people apparently tend to jump at anything at all that seems to offer a solution or a way out. This factor is then accorded the highest priority and unquestioned validity, even if the chosen reference point is completely inappropriate or would have been totally insignificant

---

[10] Erickson, Milton H. "The Confusion Technique in Hypnosis." *Selected Papers of Milton H. Erickson*. New York: Grune and Statton, 1967.

under other circumstances. It seems that in such confused situations one is particularly susceptible to any suggestions to which one is exposed at the crucial moment. What is more, such suggestions need not lead only to exhibitions of negative (paranoid) behavior; they can be put to positive (e.g., therapeutic) use as well.

However, the previously mentioned consequence of behavior in confused situations is of much greater interest for marketing—the peculiarity that on occasion these situations sharpen perception for even the smallest details.

In unusual situations, for example those of great danger, one is often capable of certain completely spontaneous responses entirely beyond the pale of everyday behavior. Without any forethought, people are apparently able on occasion to make, and act on, the most vital and complex decisions in no time at all. A good example of this are the people who are the first to help at accident scenes—people who say of themselves that they normally cannot stand to look at blood, let alone open wounds, without getting sick to the stomach. Confronted with the acute need to act, however, all of a sudden they are nevertheless able to help save lives without feelings of disgust or anxiety. It is not until later, perhaps as much as several days, that in retrospect these helpers develop a full awareness of the situation. Then, suddenly, they experience the feelings of anxiety, disgust, or even paralysis familiar to them under such circumstances.

Similar things have no doubt occurred to many people at one time or another, perhaps under less spectacular circumstances. Let us take the example of a completely everyday, routine task at your desk that you were attending to in an inattentive and absent-minded fashion. Without thinking, you open a dictionary to exactly the right place or pull just the number of copies you need from a stack of forms, as if this were the easiest thing in the world. If you tried to repeat the trick, of course, it would end in failure. The frustrating impression you get is that just your intention to repeat the process is what prevents it from succeeding.

In Far Eastern philosophies there is a large amount of literature on this topic of the unintentional attainment of goals. The Taoist concept of *wu-wei*, intentional purposelessness, comes to mind here, or the idea taught in Zen Buddhism that one has to forget what one wants to attain in order to attain it. You have no doubt also encountered this phenomenon in the frantic search in your memory for a concept, a number, or an event. As soon as you give up the search and think of something else, however, what you were trying to think of occurs to you spontaneously.

Whether or not higher spiritual abilities or transcendent energies are involved here is a question that shall be left up to you. However, it is a conspicuous and striking fact that in some situations a certain kind of *purposeless inattentiveness* does create a higher sensibility—particularly for "trivial," nonverbal interactions that can be of decisive importance in interpersonal situations and, of course, in advertising statements. Therefore, these phenomena are of interest for marketing and, in the broader sense, for the analysis of the blurred contours of what we call reality.

Chapter 12
Subtle Influencing

One researcher who has recognized the great significance of subtle influencing for communication sciences is Robert Rosenthal, who is known for his psychological experiments at Harvard that demonstrate how the various assumptions of researchers conducting experiments influence the behavior and performance of rats. This is the case even where experimenters are convinced that they have completely distanced themselves from any and all preconceptions.

Rosenthal has also studied the effects of deliberate, yet indirect influencing of persons. In one study,[11] he showed test subjects a series of photos of unknown persons. He let them guess the professional or social success of those persons on a scale of minus 10 (very unsuccessful) to plus 10 (very successful). The only grounds for the assessment were the general impressions that the photos made on the test persons. In numerous preliminary studies, the questionnaires yielded a neutral average value (zero). In other words, the persons to be evaluated were described as being neither particularly successful nor unsuccessful.

The following real tests were carried out by several experimenters. Each of them was assigned a certain value on a scale of minus 10 to plus 10. The task of each experimenter was to indirectly influence their respective test subject to choose the value assigned to that experimenter. The experiments were filmed. All the films were later shown to a substantial number of observers. The purpose of the experiment was explained to the observers, but they were not told the values that the experimenters were trying to influence their respective test subjects to choose. The test was a test of the observers' ability

---

[11]   Rosenthal, Robert. *Experimental Effects in Behavioral Research*. New York: Appleton-Century-Crofts, 1966.

to perform a certain task with respect to the filmed test. It was the task of the observers to guess—simply on the basis of their subjective feelings upon watching the films—the respective values the conductors of the experiment were to influence their test persons to choose.

Rosenthal reports that the estimates of the film viewers were, amazingly, very exact. You can imagine the importance for marketing of this experiment, as well the underlying effect of indirect and nonverbal communication. Not only animals but also we humans are clearly subject to influences of which we are not conscious and hence about which we can form no direct, conscious opinion.

Rhetoricians, for example, are, of course, aware of the obvious fact that they are not only recipients but also transmitters of such subconscious influences. However much we may try to avoid it, we are constantly influencing our fellow human beings in the most various ways without being explicitly aware of it. You certainly have had the experience of meeting a person for the first time and, without having exchanged a word, feeling repelled by this person right from the start. "I don't know what it is," you may have thought, "but something about this guy really puts me off." Your partner, on the other hand, may have thought the new acquaintance thoroughly pleasant. Perhaps subtle influences play a decisive role in these scarcely measurable spontaneous judgments as well.

Modern communication research confronts us with a problem area of which a few years ago we were not even aware: we can be the causes of influences of which we know nothing. If these influences emanating from us were always manifest, identity problems would probably be a more frequent occurrence. The fact that we exert subtle influences on those with whom we communicate—with unconscious gestures, mood swings, or other scarcely perceptible factors (just think of the ability of dolphins to register supersonic waves)—could provide an explanation for occasionally inexplicable reactions on the part of others.

The mechanisms of subtle influencing are clearly observable in the family. For here particularly close relationships obtain, and family members are minutely attuned to each other's emotional changes. In the typical forms of double binds described above, the relational aspect of the paradoxical communication is often nonverbal and indirect.

The father of an aggressive boy, for example, often exhibits two contradictory stances: on the one hand the official, critical stance, which rejects aggressiveness and insists on good behavior and respect for social norms; on the other hand, a completely different, nonverbal and indirect "approval stance," of which the father is himself perhaps not even aware. Yet at any allusion to the positive energies of his small boy or to the necessity of his being able to defend himself, the father's shining eyes and undeniable pride do not escape the attention of the onlooker, let alone the "misbehaving" son.

Sales managers also play this game. They well know how to put on a show of dressing down a field representative for being overly aggressive toward customers. Secretly, however, they appreciate the enthusiasm of the employee, as well as the good sales figures. The sales representative will most likely register the second, if contradictory, message.

A sales representative betrays himself in a similar manner if his customer puts him into a pessimistic mood or turns him off altogether. In such a situation, sales representatives will, of course, try to express themselves as positively and optimistically as possible. At the same time, however, they might well be negatively influencing the customer unconsciously and indirectly, and consequently jeopardizing the sale.

The work of Rosenthal and other researchers in the field of subtle influencing has led to considerable discussion about the modalities of this sometimes very intensive influencing. For many rationalistic persons, this issue seems somewhat esoteric and hence unworthy of discussion. But what is involved here goes far beyond what is ordinarily understood as subtle influencing. This is clearly shown by the experimentally established fact of being able to influence test subjects, indirectly and without their knowledge, to the extent of causing them to make accurate estimates on a 10-point scale. This fact seems anything but esoteric, although some might be inclined to explain such real phenomena with supersensory energies, cosmic rays, or other supernatural articles of faith.

Subtle influences are not bizarre miracles but rather plain matters of fact. In present-day hypnotherapy, for example, it has been observed that the use of hypnosis can have dangerous effects if the hypnotist thinks that the use of hypnosis can in fact lead to dangerous consequences.

Modern marketers regularly attempt to utilize the effects of subtle influencing. Particularly in the United States, not only visual but also auditory means have been employed. In supermarkets, customers were at one time bombarded with virtually inaudible suggestions to buy. Certain brand names were incessantly repeated over the PA system and thus subliminally hammered into the unconscious of the unsuspecting customer. The success was so great that consumer organizations got completely up in arms. The result was that this extreme form of influencing consumers was forbidden by law.

Eckhard H. Hess is also a proponent of the long and hotly disputed assumptions about subtle influencing. As is so often the case with interesting discoveries, the catalyst for the work done by Hess was a coincidental event. "About five years ago I was reading in bed one evening and leafing through a book with conspicuously beautiful animal photos. My wife happened to glance over and mentioned that the light must be too poor because the pupils of my eyes were unusually wide. It seemed to me that the bedside lamp was certainly bright enough. I told her as much but she insisted that my pupils were widened." [12] Prompted by this event to experiment, Hess later found out that the size of the pupil does not, in fact, depend merely on the strength of the light striking it but also on the emotional state of the person in question.

In lyric poetry it has been well known for centuries that emotional states can be expressed through the eyes. Familiar poetic formulations like "cold glances filled with hatred," or "their glances overflowed with love and happiness" refer to the fact that in certain situations persons unconsciously send out these minimal signals, or are influenced by them without being aware of it. Hess proved that this phenomenon is more than just a matter of poetic formulations and metaphors. He established in the course of his research that certain conjurers, for example, closely observe changes in the size of the pupils of their counterparts and draw conclusions from these observations. If a card that the volunteer was supposed to remember is laid in front of a card-trick artist, in some cases the pupils of the volunteer widen. It has been reported that Chinese jade dealers could determine from observing the dilations of the pupil of their customers the degree of interest in their goods. From this they could infer the article for which the customer would pay the highest price.

A further experiment done by Hess is also very interesting in this connection: He showed test subjects two photos of a pretty young woman. Since they had been taken from the same negative, the two pictures were absolutely identical. There was only one minimal difference: in one of the two pictures the pupils of the portrayed woman had been retouched so as to slightly widen them. Hess found that the reaction to the retouched photo with the widened pupils was more than twice as strong. After the experiment the test subjects declared unanimously that the two pictures seemed identical to them. Some did say, however, that they thought the one picture was "more feminine," "prettier" or "softer." But none of the test persons directly noticed the retouching of the pupil size.

Already in the Middle Ages women in high society were using a preparation known as "belladonna" (Italian for "beautiful woman") to widen their pupils. Dilated pupils seemed to have a more appealing, or erotic effect, at least on men. Perhaps dilated pupils signal to males a higher degree of interest on the part of the woman.

---

[12]   Hess, Eckhard H. "Attitude and Pupil Size." *Scientific American* 212 (1965):46–54.

So far, the phenomenon of subtle forms of human communication has been only superficially studied, probably because of the erroneous association with irrational and esoteric phenomena. However, there is considerable evidence that the example of pupil dilation is but one merely of many nonverbal and subconscious forms of behavior that constantly influence—if not control—interpersonal relationships.

Chapter 13

Individualized Causality

"I have trained this human being to the point that he gives me really top quality food every time I push against this lever with my nose! Aren't humans clever?"

Perhaps you know this old joke about the laboratory rat explaining to its colleagues the astonishing behavior of the experimenter.

Here one and the same stimulus-response sequence is involved. But from each of the two different perspectives, or frames of reference, involved—that of the rat or that of the human being—a completely different, contradictory conclusion is drawn and subsequently generalized into a law. The scientific experimenter interprets the lever pressure of the rat unequivocally as a learned response to a stimulus previously provoked by the experimenter. The rat, on the other hand, understands the reality of the situation quite differently. For the rat, the lever pressure is also causal, but from the rat's point of view it is the experimenter who has been prompted and who then always responds obediently by handing out food.

This *individualized causality*, as I would like to call it, is one of the main causes of difficulties in interpersonal communications. In advertising, individualized causality can become a dangerous trap for the seller, such as when a response from the perspective of the person being addressed is falsely assessed. In Part Three, which proposes communicational solutions, additional examples will be provided to illustrate these relationships.

Both parties—the human being and the rat—have understood exactly the same facts. But they nevertheless attach completely different meanings to them. One can speak here of two completely different views of reality. If we applied this model to interpersonal relationships, then it is highly probable that each of the parties involved would declare the other to be insane.

From a communicational point of view, the key to the elimination or avoidance of difficulties in interpersonal relationships might well lie simply in the clarification of the communicational fundamentals involved. Individualized causality is a nasty trap. Often the parties entangled in this elementary pattern are unable to extricate themselves by their own efforts. A quick "tip" provided by a third party can work miracles: "You both use the same words but you are nevertheless talking about two completely different things." The opposite case should also be familiar. Here the exact same thing is talked about or the standpoint is identical. But the respective formulation of these identical positions creates the impression of completely different standpoints.

Do you recall the various modalities of communicational punctuation? Punctuation assumes the function here of collating viewpoints with an individual frame of reference. You can well imagine the existential significance of this function—for without the development of certain individual frames of reference, our own world would appear to us as chaotic, directionless, and unpredictable. Albert Einstein once put forward the thesis: "The theory determines what we are able to observe. I have little patience with scientists who take a board, look for the thinnest part of it, and then drill a bunch of holes at the place where it takes the least effort to drill."[13]

In human relationships, however, the theory (here, the "punctuation") is itself the product and hence the result of a preceding punctuation. Here is where an error can frequently be observed in interpersonal conflicts, or in the assessment of target groups in marketing. It is simply overlooked, or intentionally ignored, depending on the case, that every participant in a communicational process has systematized his intercommunicational view of reality in a manner differing from, or contradictory to, that of the other. This fact can result in the curious and erroneous generalization from one's own mind-set that there is only one reality and hence only one appropriate view of reality—namely one's own.

The subjective view can thus arise among the parties involved that the respective other must be pathological, schizophrenic, or malicious—for the other party sees the true state of affairs quite differently, i.e., wrongly. The two parties involved speak two different languages. One can compare them with software programmers who use totally different programming languages and nevertheless try to create a program together. Their endeavor is doomed to failure from the outset.

---

[13]   Frank, Philip. "Einstein's Philosophy of Science." *Reviews of Modern Physics* vol. 21, no. 3 (1949).

A study from the 1950s shows clearly that the dilemma of confusion in interpersonal relationships is the direct consequence of different views of reality on the part of the intercommunicators. Toward the end of World War II, thousands of American GIs on their way to Europe paid a short visit to Great Britain. This phenomenon created ideal conditions for a sociological study of British culture, which was subsequently subjected to an out-and-out mass movement. It is easy to see that in this situation—particularly at that time—two worlds came into collision with each other. A study was made of the structures of the resulting relationships between young American men and young British women. Interestingly enough, the results from the numerous interviews showed exactly the same reproach from both sides: both the American soldiers and the British girls accused each other of unpleasant tactlessness in sexual matters.

The situation becomes more intelligible if approached from the communicational perspective—i.e., as a problem of punctuation. The culturally conditioned sequence in the development of new relationships—here from first getting to know one another up to sexual intercourse—passes through roughly the same number of ritual behavior patterns in the case both of American men and British women. The decisive point here, however, is the sequence of these patterns, for this sequence is completely different in the two cultures. The American soldier puts the act of kissing, for example, at about the relatively early Step 5. He understands the kiss, regardless of how passionate, as completely harmless and, above all, as entailing no obligation. For the British woman, on the other hand, the kiss is already regarded as a very erotic act and therefore occupies a much later position—i.e., Step 25—in the development of a relationship.

When the American assumed the time had come for an "innocent" kiss, the British woman found this approach anything but innocent; she judged it rather to be totally premature, obtrusive behavior that she couldn't accept at this early stage of the relationship. For her, the question was now already raised of immediately breaking off the budding relationship or surrendering herself sexually to her boyfriend. (This, namely, was what would now have to be decided according to her cultural sequence.)

If she opted for the second alternative, on the assumption of doing exactly as her boyfriend wanted, the American GI would most likely have understood this as shameless, since in terms of his ritual frame of reference the relationship was at a much too early stage for sexual contacts.

Now at this point we could make the typical mistake of judging the individual behavior of the girl in isolation from the communicational laws of punctuation. It wouldn't be difficult for us to make a psychoanalytical diagnosis here. If she precipitously breaks off the relationship after the first kiss and beats a hasty retreat, then this could be interpreted as hysterical behavior. If on the other hand she starts to undress, then this would seem like nymphomania.

It can hardly be emphasized too strongly that here, as well as in many similar communication patterns, conflicts are involved that cannot be reduced causally to one of the two parties. They are rather conflicts that lie exclusively in the nature of the relationship and the type of interaction.

Misinformation frequently arises in interpersonal relationships, as well as in the formulation of advertising messages, because the parties involved fail to recognize the decisive interpersonal nature of the conflict. The problem behind these misjudgments and conflicts is the communication process itself or the ignorance about its laws. Ludwig Wittgenstein formulates this state of misinformation very aptly: "What we cannot think, we cannot think; therefore we cannot say what we cannot think, either."[14]

In the late 1950s, a strange "epidemic" broke out in a small town in the United States. More and more car owners noticed when they got into their cars in the morning that their windshields were covered with tiny scratches. Within a short time two theories about the scratched windshields were in circulation among the residents of the town. Many annoyed drivers were firmly convinced that Russian nuclear tests had contaminated the air. The radioactive rain produced by this had been transformed into a corrosive precipitation that was now eating away at the glass of the windshields. A second group thought that they could demonstrate unequivocally that drops of acid from long stretches of freshly asphalted freeways had been splashing against windshields and scratching them to pieces, a process that had been aggravated further by the very damp air in the town.

However, a state fact-finding committee by no means started their work with an investigation of the two suggestions. They concentrated their efforts rather on trying to ascertain if the assertion of an increase in badly scratched windshields could be confirmed at all. It turned out that in the entire town no increase whatsoever in badly scratched windshields could be objectively determined. None of the windshields was more and or less scratched, in keeping with their age, than were the windshields of other cars elsewhere in the world.

Here we have a cardinal example of the way in which mass behavior, once it gets started, develops a virulent internal dynamic of individualized causality, pulling along others in its wake. Keep in mind that the reports in town of damaged windshields kept piling up. It is clear that thereupon almost all drivers examined their cars for damage. They quite naturally did a thorough

---

[14]   Wittgenstein, Ludwig. *Tractatus Logico-Philosophicus*: 5.61.

job of checking their windshields. They bent over the windshields with a critical eye and looked at them up close. Even in the case of a brand new vehicle, one probably would find some kind of scratch with this procedure if one tried hard enough.

This sensational event in the small American town was by no means an epidemic of scratched windshields or the underhanded attack of a militant anti-car party. The real explanation for the "phenomenon" was far more mundane. Hence, the media, which had previously reacted with outrage and joined in the speculations, responded, as is so often the case with spectacular world events that turn out to be flops, with the infamous tactic of hushing up the entire windshield story.

Such cases could give rise to the nasty suspicion that top stories like the AIDS panic, mad-cow disease, national bankruptcies, disastrous economic forecasts, or other apocalyptic prophecies also have their origin in similar mechanisms. Clearly even completely trivial, insignificant incidents or circumstances easily lend themselves to being combined with emotionally loaded subjects. From this point on, an avalanche of opinion is triggered that no longer requires even the slightest additional proofs or confirmations. A mechanism is set in motion that constantly confirms and reinforces itself. In extreme cases, such a development can progress to the point where no one looks for a causal connection anymore but simply accepts the stories in circulation as gospel truth.

What an ideal state of affairs for the positioning of your products and services!

One can appreciate, therefore, what enormous effects individualized communicational punctuation can have. It is not a question of psychology. It is a question of your personal or entrepreneurial communication and the knowledge of the laws.

Chapter 14
The Tone Makes the Music: Punctuation

The question of whether and how far our behavior is the product of subtle influences is best left up to each individual to judge by herself on the basis of her own observations and experiences. At any rate, most everyone agrees that the primary role of language is that of a medium for conveying meaning. This takes us into the field of semantics.

From the perspective of communication science, unequivocal indications (which do not necessarily have to be directly connected with each other) of how a given sequence of words is to be punctuated are indispensable for the understanding of these words. In other words, the meaning of a statement can remain unintelligible if the complementing or documenting punctuation is lacking.

Consider the following example: *"Do you think that that's beautiful?"*

This statement can have completely different meanings depending on the emphasis put on the respective words. The meaning of the sentence "Do *you* think that that's beautiful?" is different from the meaning of the sentence "Do you think that *that's* beautiful?" Yet in both cases we are dealing with the same six words.

Another example is the old children's joke "I have ten digits on each hand, five and twenty on my hands and feet." The correct punctuation would, of course, be: "I have ten digits—on each hand five, and twenty on my hands and feet."

Written language provides numerous tools for the expression of semantic punctuation. These consist first of all in the instruments comprised in the dictionary definition of "punctuation," i.e., grammatical punctuation marks, such as the period, comma, question mark, etc. To these should be added typographical emphasis, such as underlining, bold type, italics, etc. Unusual symbols and onomatopoetic devices, which occur particularly frequently in comic-book language, also belong here—e.g., the skull and crossbones, the hangman's noose, the ax, ink blots, thick exclamation marks for "unspeakably crude curses," or the gulp of Donald Duck.

Indeed, the manifold possibilities of semantic punctuation in spoken language are far greater than those of the written word. Spoken language offers innumerable paralingual variations, such as tone of voice, interjections, coughs, sighs, laughter, rate of speech, volume. Nevertheless, written punctuation does offer a broad range of possibilities as well. Exclamation marks and quotation marks, for example, serve not only to avoid but also to provoke ambiguities. The potential of these limited, apparently weak devices is often underestimated. For this reason they are a popular means of communicating allusions or hidden messages. A good example is the following statement from the job reference of a butcher's apprentice who was not always impeccably honest: "He is honest, down to the bones."

The next example, taken from the marketing practices of a particular sect, is much more grave. You will see in this example how it is possible, again, by changing the position of a single punctuation mark, to turn the worldview of millions of people upside down. You will learn about a marketing crime story that may well be without parallel.

The Jehovah's Witnesses have developed a strategy that demonstrates in an exemplary fashion how a single grammatical sign, namely the colon, can pervert the biblical interpretation of reality to such an extent that, on the basis of the understanding thus generated, an entirely new, different reality is created—a reality that quite apparently functions as intended confusion within the context of the sect's strategy.

This concerns the biblical passage (Luke 23:43) in which Jesus hangs dying on the cross and explains to the remorseful criminal crucified along with him that he will enter into paradise with Jesus that very day: "Truly, I say to you, today you will be with me in Paradise."[15] One conclusion drawn from this statement down through the ages by all of Christendom has been that there is a life immediately after death. The ingenious Bible experts of the Jehovah's Witnesses use a grammatical trick to disprove this hopeful inference. They claim that in this passage, as in many others, the Bible has been incorrectly translated. For what Christ really said is, "Truly, I say to you today, you will be with me in Paradise."

Note the placement of the comma after the word *today.* In the opinion of the Jehovah's Witnesses, the word "today" refers simply to the temporal determination of the formulation of the statement and not to the time of the entry into Paradise.

---

[15]   St. Luke's Gospel: 23:43.

You might well be wondering what the point of this grammatical hairsplitting is. A closer examination of the strategic goals and rhetorical methods of this very widespread sect, however, will quickly reveal the point of the confusion consciously produced by using different punctuation. The idea that a person who sincerely repents will receive mercy and be forgiven, as depicted in the Christian understanding of the Bible, coincides by no means with the worldview of this particular sect. According to the doctrines and so-called biblical guidelines of the Jehovah's Witnesses, a substantial part of the meaning of life consists in convincing other people of the precepts and doctrines of God (whereby God is designated only as Jehovah—another intentional rhetorical device)—for only if a person follows these laws for an entire lifetime (which for the most part really are in accord with the Christian view of the Bible) will they survive Armageddon, which is a kind of Last Judgment in which the good are rewarded and the wicked are punished.

If the sect were to accept modern biblical interpretation, such as the interpretation in the above-described case of repentance and forgiveness on the Cross, they would have difficulty motivating their obedient flock to preach at people's front doors, as well as taking other castigating privations upon themselves. For according to the Christian view of a kind, forgiving, and nonpunitive deity, God grants us the freedom to experience the world, make wrong decisions, and repent them, to the end that every sinner has the possibility of ultimately attaining the Kingdom of Heaven. This stands in glaring contrast to the life of a Jehovah's Witness—a life characterized by penitence and penance as a necessary condition for gaining admission to the small circle of the elect.

It is indeed interesting to note the significant consequences a single comma can have, in this case even to the extent of inverting the basic understanding of a world religion.

Due to their worldwide distribution (several million members), the Jehovah's Witnesses have become an institution to be taken seriously. For a long time, they have been a source of irritation to mainstream denominations. Of particular interest is the circumstance that so far it has been impossible to refute the good and magnanimous purpose emphasized by the members. To this day, dozens of theologians around the world ask themselves, "What is really behind this? There must be a catch to it somewhere..." The marketing practices of other groups, like Scientology or Bhagwan, make them easier targets for the criticism of church experts on sectarianism. Sooner or later, a guru representing nothing but his own material self-interests steps out of his golden temple—a guru who exerts systematic control over his or her disciples and exploits them financially. To this day, however, there has been no indication that the Jehovah's Witnesses have such structures. They seem to constitute a self-powered communication model that preserves and perpetuates itself solely on the basis of its clear-cut, authoritarian structures.

However, the personal problems of the dropouts from the Jehovah's Witnesses alone provide grounds for a critical discussion of this group of biblical acrobats. To some extent, the dropouts are avoided like leprous traitors by the sect members, even if they are not threatened directly, as is the case with militant sects.

After conducting several intensive interviews with ex-members, I came up with some interesting findings. All of those questioned were unanimously glad to have succeeded in liberating themselves from the community, in some cases even in the face of extremely hefty family resistance. All of them cite as the primary motivation for leaving the imposition of numerous obligations which were always declared to be voluntary. (Note the paradox of "voluntary obligation.") For these ex-members, the anxieties connected with the various compulsions increased to an unbearable point. These anxieties were generated by the *mechanism of conscience pangs*, a tried-and-true, time-honored method in the history of dogmatic systems.

What was repeatedly designated as the main problem was the anxiety about not being able to enter into Paradise if one did not live in accordance with the allegedly biblical view of reality. These anxieties will perhaps seem trivial or naive to an uninvolved reader who lives in accordance with their own personal worldview. But before making such a judgment, it should be kept in mind that one's personal view of reality affects one's own behavior in vastly more trivial situations. After all, the issue involved here concerns one of life's most central questions, one which everyone has struggled with at some point: what happens after death?

The Jehovah's Witnesses offer quite simple solutions to just these fundamental questions of human existence—solutions that seem plausible and, with a little imagination, biblically verifiable as well. The strategy of the sect is implemented with the awareness that it wins over new converts with the offer of solutions strategically formulated by a particular kind of punctuation, even if from another point of view these solutions are nothing but far-fetched illusions. New converts do not see themselves being motivated to become adherents by intrapsychic problems, i.e., problems within themselves. They rather succumbed to the fallacy of thinking that they could embark on a new path that would enable them to define a new (and better) reality.

The interviews yielded the following result: The effects of the influencing strategy are so far-reaching that even former members (including some respectable academics) who had dissociated themselves from the organization years earlier still had occasional doubts about the correctness of their decision.

The main question they ask themselves is whether they might, in fact, fail to pass through Armageddon and thus miss out on eternal life.

Here, again, the significance of language and intercommunication at the relational level is manifest. Nowhere can language be employed with greater possibilities of misunderstanding than in marketing. This book is by no means intended to be a critical sociological analysis of religious sects. Nevertheless, the techniques and intercommunicational models of the Jehovah's Witnesses in particular seem particularly noteworthy. For this sect succeeds more than do others in winning over not only disoriented individuals but also intelligent, "respectable" people who are firmly anchored in life.

The fact that the strategic employment of communication can fill millions of people with so much enthusiasm for something is in itself well worth closer inspection—for marketing is the constant attempt to convince people effectively. And this sect does an astonishingly good job of convincing people.

What businessman is not keenly interested in learning what techniques would put him in a position to convince thousands of people of his products or services? We will now discuss how opinions, views, and worldviews arise in the minds of those one is trying to reach.

Chapter 15
Order and Meaning

Long before the emergence of psychology and modern sciences communication, questions of punctuation in the broader sense were receiving attention in literature, particularly in dramas and comedies.

Already in the literature of antiquity, conflicts and intrigues that could end with the mutual slaughter of entire families were a popular theme. In classical drama, the central plot was constituted by conflicting views of reality and the ensuing impossibility for the protagonists of deciding which was the legitimate viewpoint. The virtually infinite variety of punctuation was a favorite device of writers, poets, and comedians for depicting paradoxes and chaos, which usually did not get resolved until the conclusion of the story.

It would seem that in our own way, we each attempt to give meaning to the occurrences and events taking place around them. Even if this search takes place unconsciously, it is nevertheless always in process. On any given day, as soon as any one of the many impressions that surround and impinge upon us succeeds in circumventing the defense mechanisms in the brain and receiving attention, we first ponder the meaning of the impression, or at least a review the facts of the matter. This search does not concern meaning in the philosophical and existential sense of the word but rather the significance or simply the utility of events taking place around us daily, events which are more or less tragic or trivial.

Some contemporaries have a particularly strong tendency to suspect the workings of a higher power behind even the most insignificant events and experiences of everyday life. It seems to be part of the essence of human nature to keep searching for an underlying scheme of things. This search has considerable consequences which do not exactly tend to make life easier and less complicated.

You have probably said, on a suitable occasion, "This always happens (only) to me," although you were fully aware of the fact that the repetition of fateful or even trivial events in your life is merely the result of chance. If a certain event repeats itself often enough, or just gives some indication of a certain sequence, there is the temptation to think—if only for a moment—that one has discovered a certain pattern and therefore an explanation. This phenomenon results in the following perception: "This always happens only to me. This cannot just be a coincidence anymore. There's something behind this."

One could no doubt be tempted to dismiss as mere quirks these situations in which one grasps at illusory solutions. But the underlying communicational mechanism is of the greatest significance for commercial and personal marketing. The search for a self-defined order in the course of events is ultimately nothing other than a manifestation of individual punctuation. If this individual punctuation manifests itself more strongly, for example, by further events, then the view of reality in question can become self-fulfilling simply by virtue of the concentrated attention on just these events.

The notion of a self-fulfilling prophecy is primarily familiar in a negative context. It is a "mystery" that can turn into reality if intimations, anxieties, or doubts are repeatedly spoken out loud or formulated in the mind. They finally do occur as a result of constantly visualizing and imagining their reality. Overanxious parents, for example, have to reckon with the possibility that they expose their children to risks that otherwise might never have materialized if their overly worried parents hadn't constantly drawn attention to the many pitfalls in life. We have all heard of traffic accidents after which the victims report that they had already had a strong feeling of malaise upon starting their trip. It seems as if states of anxiety and phobias can be communicated to other persons and undermine their sense of security to such an extent that precisely that event occurs that was feared in the first place.

Typical patterns are:

- "The traffic light is always red when I drive along this street."
- "Every Sunday I drop the coffee filter when you start to get on my nerves."
- "I just don't get along with people who were born under the same sign of the Zodiac that I was."
- "I never make any sales on Monday."

However, with concentrated mental training, it is also possible to generate *positive* self-fulfilling prophecies by visualizing desired conditions. One good technique for this is neurolinguistic programming (NLP).

A fundamental objective of modern marketing based on communicational findings consists in activating the mechanisms involved in the search for meaning. The great—one can even say, the fantastic mystical—advantage of an identification generated "pseudoinformally" on this basis consists in its manifest durability.

Try some time to convince a superstitious person of the erroneousness of their superstitiousness. If the attempt is successful at all, then it is only with the help of the strategic means of metacommunication. In the course of maintaining their "belief" over the years, the superstitious person has built up numerous effective mechanisms that deny the rejection of their view of reality. A worldview based on this form of the "innate striving for order" is almost incontrovertible.

What this means for communicational marketing is that once a company or product has been positioned in the minds of consumers by means of interactive communication, it is an extremely difficult task to supplant it. The pertinent question at this juncture concerns the means required for attaining such a position. The communicational mode of access to the frame of reference of those being addressed—i.e., potential customers—is explained concretely and in detail in Part Three. The first step consists in making oneself, one's product, or one's company the object of a search for order on the part of those being addressed. To this end, it is necessary to ascertain what type of order is being sought for in any given case, and in order to make this determination it is essential to identify the worldview, or mind-set, of the target group.

It will not always be possible to determine the nature of something as existentially meaningful as the search for order, let alone find solutions for it. But the existence of a natural, innate striving for order does seem apparent.

The knowledge of all of the fundamental features of human behavior we have discussed will in itself be of great help to you in planning your marketing strategy, and perhaps in your personal relationships as well. If you have a better understanding of the way communication works, you can position yourself much more effectively in conflict situations. You can employ your resources with a clearer view of you objective and thus to a greater effect.

Part 2 Summary

Human communication is complex. Not surprisingly, confusion can arise. An essential objective of advertising consists in getting attention. From a psychological perspective, almost every means that serves the attainment of this objective is worth considering. But as was shown in the case of the telecommunications provider, massive confusion can lead to rejection of the advertising message.

Communicational double binds arise when two mutually exclusive rhetorical alternatives are offered. In most cases, the response of the person entangled in a double bind is to attempt to withdraw from the communicational situation.

A communication pattern that can frequently be observed in advertising is the "Be spontaneous!" paradox. The person addressed is prompted to do something that can only occur spontaneously—i.e., without being prompted. Hence, all enjoinments in advertisements should be examined for this problem.

The consequences of the "Be spontaneous!" paradox in advertising messages are illustrated by the CIP Pyramid. As a rule, the consequence of this pattern is that the consumer turns the original inducement into its opposite.

An unpleasant side effect of subtle influencing is the difficulty of avoiding it. Nevertheless, it clearly exists for all that and has a considerable impact.

When we become entangled in paradoxes, or when we simply cannot find any direct way out of a strange situation, we tend to fall back upon already existing parallels in our system of reference. We termed this phenomenon "individualized causality."

The third and final part of this book will show how you can put all of this knowledge about communication to work in your own marketing strategies.

Part 3

Communicational Marketing

How many disputes could have been reduced to a marginal note if the opponents had dared to define their concepts clearly.

—Aristotle

Chapter 16

Communicational Marketing: A New Approach

Communication versus Psychology

The first two parts of this book show how certain forms of behavior arise and how, in their various manifestations, they affect the behavior of others. It is true that psychology and psychoanalysis also engage in similar pursuits. In these disciplines, however, the subject matter is constituted by the individual person and intrapsychic phenomena. On the basis of the results obtained, a certain conception of the human being—psychological conception—is then postulated.

All of us have been influenced in schools and universities to a greater or lesser extent by a conception of man characterized by psychological terminology. This influence is so widespread that concepts, such as "subconscious," "conditioning," "phobia," "depression," and "psychosis" have entered into everyday language.

One of the primary objectives of marketing is to influence people. It is always difficult to understand this statement in an unbiased manner. The term *influencing* is immediately associated with concepts like manipulation, control, dictatorship, etc. This perception no doubt comes from past and present experiences with dictatorial systems. By means of sophisticated propaganda techniques, these systems succeed in inducing entire populations to engage in ethically reprehensible behavior.

Although the unbiased consideration of the concept of "influencing" seems highly problematic, the use of this concept is nevertheless necessary if a reasonably matter-of-fact discussion of this topic is to be possible at all. The critical reader might note that a critical attitude toward the topic of exerting influence corresponds to a certain reality, namely her own: by communicating just this reality to others, she herself exerts a certain influence. Thus, given a certain prerequisite, the subject of exerting influence can indeed be treated in an unbiased fashion. This prerequisite is the restriction of ethical and moral value judgments to the respective intention.

Similar to the case of the religious scientist in chapter 6, an objective treatment of topics that can touch upon morally sensitive areas is possible only from a metacommunicational perspective.

Formerly, it seemed like a good idea for marketing to make use of the many valuable results of psychology and psychoanalysis—which were intended to define the human being and his or her individual behavior— as an instrumentality for influencing customers, employees, suppliers, or the media. The starting point was the typical scientific and pragmatic assumption: if it can be explained how a particular thing works (such as human psychology) then it is a simple matter to influence this thing or even control it. Out of this idea were developed innumerable sales techniques, rhetorical devices, and suggestion techniques for bombarding the center of human consciousness or subconscious. It became apparent in the 1960s that in the Western industrial nations massive overproduction had created certain market saturations. Thereupon, more and more sophisticated "sales methods" were developed. These methods sounded very convincing on the basis of their psychological explanations, but they did not always attain the hoped-for success nevertheless.

To this very day, psychology and its results (obtained primarily from experiments with pathologically disturbed subjects) remain the foundation of marketing strategies. The successes of even the most elaborate advertising campaigns, supported by million-dollar budgets, are often only modest. This gives rise to the suspicion that the purely psychological approach is wrong-headed: too many highly relevant factors are simply ignored. Parts 1 and 2 of this book demonstrated that psychology—propagated as the intellectual foundation of marketing—is itself caught in dilemmas that result precisely from the view of the human being described above.

In light of the foregoing, it would seem an urgently necessary task to refocus on the fact that the human being is not merely an organic and psychological entity, but to a very great extent an interdependent, communicative being. In this—social—context completely different and farther-reaching laws obtain than those that govern the individual human psyche.

The Competent Consumer

In view of the findings attained in communication science and the mechanisms that have been ascertained here, the author calls for a paradigm switch in modern marketing in the discussion of behavior and the means of influencing it. It is time to leave behind the one-sided, purely psychological approach of the 1950s and 1960s. This appeal is directed not only to advertising strategists who imagine that they can manipulate the subconscious of the customer simply by extolling the virtues of the product in a sufficiently suggestive fashion; it is also directed to the entrepreneur who is supposed to finance this mistaken approach.

In the following exposition, the contrasting orientations of these two positions will be designated (for better semantic differentiability) as classical *psychological marketing,* on the one hand, and modern *communicational marketing* on the other.

One fundamental element of communicational marketing is the conviction that human beings are not simply a product of their own individual psyche. With respect to their behavior they most definitely exist in a relationship of interdependence with their social environment.

A further premise is that the consumer is an intelligent, competent person who erects communicational defense mechanisms against external "attacks," similar to the way in which humans have developed physical defense mechanisms against environmental influences. Whoever is not prepared to accord human beings this fundamental characteristic of individual competence will have difficulty grasping most of the material in this book. The problems connected with the disposition of immature, easily manipulated individuals and their consequences require no further elucidation here.

On the basis of these considerations, *communicational marketing* is here defined as a new approach. In order to understand this approach, the psychological perspective has to be put in brackets for a moment. Become aware of the social and interrelational elements in human behavior which are subject to the laws of communication and start to incorporate these into your marketing approach.

Communicational marketing means understanding the other person (employee, customer, business friend) as a *competent communication partner* whose behavior is decisively characterized by his or her respective worldview. Forget the widespread attempt to manipulate the human being through the psyche. This classic marketing technique is not only questionable from a moral standpoint; given the reality of communicational laws and effective defense mechanisms, this technique is ultimately doomed to failure in any case.

The following chapters offer no patent methodological remedies (like those in the presentations of demagogic marketing gurus) for communicational marketing. It is left up to sales trainers, telephone-marketing lecturers, and advertising consultants to develop their own illustrative models on the basis of the communicational approach presented in this book.

Now that the laws of communication have been elucidated, you are in a position to develop your own communicational marketing strategy, whether for your company, your individual career, or simply for a better understanding of interpersonal relationships. In the following chapters, some of the application areas of communicational marketing are discussed. Chapters 17 through 22 deal with communicational marketing vis-à-vis *the customer*—that is, the "main object" of sales-related efforts.

You shall see that one of the main problems in our efforts at communication can be communication itself. Chapter 23 focuses on *intra-company organization* with regard to communicational mechanisms. In chapter 24, the *personal communicational marketing* of the individual sales representative is discussed. And finally, in chapter 25 we review an interaction blueprint for communicational marketing.

Chapter 17
Communicating with the Customer

Avenues of Approach

Our world is anything but always logical. In most situations it seems more like a paradoxical affair. But as has been shown in Part Two, with some understanding of communicational relationships a certain inner logic can be discovered in the paradox itself. This is even true of logic that makes the paradox self-perpetuating in pathological individuals or that leads to seemingly insoluble conflicts in interpersonal relations.

Three fundamental factors from the communicational perspective can be identified in marketing. These factors are similarly postulated by "psychological marketing" as well. But in the implementation of psychological advertising strategies, these factors are either misjudged or lost sight of altogether. Let's examine them individually.

The Credibility of Statements

For classical advertising strategists, it seems to be a fundamental tenet that only the credibility of a statement—be it a simple statement of fact, an appeal, a wish, or a request—gives it meaning and qualifies it to be understood or complied with. Classical psychological marketing is based on the premise that it is possible to achieve credibility in advertising statements by analyzing what is credible for the target group and then offering it in an appropriately reinforcing manner. This method is reinforced by the employment of suggestive techniques. Thus, one proceeds from the stock assumption that the depiction of certain roles (mother, housewife, athlete, young female entrepreneur) in a commercial has a positive effect on the corresponding target group. The hoped-for identification effect is intended, among other things, to suggest credibility.

But people know how to shield themselves very effectively against these forms of suggestive attacks. The digital, or informational, statement is of no great significance with respect to credibility, if not completely irrelevant. You will recall that chapter 3 discussed the informational and relational aspects of communication. Remember that the communicatively competent person is always able to perceive a message on the relational level as well.

This means that receivers are constantly relativizing the decisive aspects of an advertising message, regardless of how suggestive, reinforcing, and technically elaborate the transmission might be. For at the relational level, it is clear to the recipient in the communicational situation that the matter at hand is just that—an advertisement. And at the relational level, advertising triggers the warning "I'd better watch out—they want something from me!" And most often, the target is not all that wrong.

Psychologically oriented advertising strategists are aware of this, of course. But they try to circumvent the relational level with the same means that produce these forms of communication in the first place. That is to say that here again they try to *not* communicate.

A recent TV ad by the Japanese automobile manufacturer Toyota provides a good example. This highly amusing, rhetorically aggressive commercial opens with Toyota's motto "Nothing is impossible!" The concluding part is introduced with the remark "And now back to the advertisement!" The attempt is made to suggest that the commercial that had just been sent is not advertising at all but rather an editorial contribution intended simply to provide information.

Here it is clearly being assumed that the human being is a naive consumer who needs only to be told what to believe. The reaction to this technique, however, will be similar to that to the pseudo-hospitality proclaimed by the hotel advertisement in chapter 9. Viewers of the Toyota ad will not be prepared go along with this paradox of a "self-negating advertising statement." Instead, they will do just the opposite and put the entire message in question. The person being addressed is confronted with the following paradox: "This is advertising, but it shouldn't be understood as such!" Viewers will sidestep the paradox by rejecting the ad sooner than buying a Toyota.

At this point, the question might be raised as to how, from the communicational perspective, credibility can be conveyed. The answer is very simple. Forget it! In advertising statements, *advantages* have to be conveyed. What your customers are always asking themselves is, "What's in it for me?" Credibility isn't an advantage that can be conveyed. Credibility either happens or it does not. If you make credibility the *theme* of your advertising statement, no one will believe a single word anymore. Credibility is like trust. The formulation of it is, at the same time, an enjoinment to make a spontaneous response.

Imagine the following scenario. All of a sudden, and for no apparent reason, your loved one starts declaring his or her faithfulness. You might well be pleased with the first declaration of fidelity. However, the third, fourth, or fifth time you will probably start wondering what's going on.

Here, as well, the original intention turns into its opposite—the CIP Pyramid. Therefore, the best strategy is to give up on an advertising message of "credibility." At the relational level the message is read like this: "Whoever tries to convey credibility must have doubts about their products. Otherwise, they wouldn't put so much emphasis on it."

Addressing Existing Needs

This heading designates a second and very popular objective in modern marketing. An erroneous assumption still widespread in marketing is that needs can be generated. But needs are not simply the product of all the various artificial fashion trends. They are based on real, specific supply shortages. A need cannot be blueprinted on a drawing board or at the CAD station of a designer or product manager. A need arises only when a supply shortage develops.

A good illustration of this can be taken from biology. In metabolic physiology, so-called *minimum factors* are identified. A minimum factor is one of a group of elements or substances necessary for successful biological development. Let us take the example of plant growth. For the growth of a plant, three minimum factors are required: water, oxygen, and nitrogen. If one of these substances is completely withheld from the plant, growth stops altogether. This remains the case even if the amount of one of the other two substances is increased. If the plant receives too little nitrogen or oxygen, no amount of additional water can increase its growth. However, if the system lacks nitrogen and this substance is added, then growth will resume or increase.

In human beings minimum factors which determine specific needs can be identified as well. The art of communicational marketing consists in the efficient identification of shortages in these minimum factors. The attempt to artificially create needs with suggestive psychological tricks leads to paradoxes that targeted consumers will ward off with their natural defense mechanisms.

The physical capabilities of a plant provide it with no defense against an oversupply of a substance; given too much water, for example, the plant would simply "drown." Some animals can defend themselves with their instinctive aggression, which manifests itself in a manner consonant with the respective species. It is hardly conceivable that a zookeeper could force additional food upon a large predatory cat that was absolutely satiated. The attempt to force-feed a fully fed predator would soon turn the initial rejection into a reaction of great confusion. Then an extremely aggressive reaction on the part of the animal would have to be reckoned with. It is apparently a characteristic of ecological systems in nature to "content" themselves with the satisfaction of minimum factors.

In addition to aggression, healthy human beings possess additional, civilized means of communication with which they can block off all offers that oversupply their already satisfied minimum factors. These are regarded as attacks that are sidestepped with communicational means. Aggression can also be employed as a defense mechanism against such suggestions. This is illustrated, for example, by the behavior of an aggressive youth generally considered to be mean and ungrateful, whose parents "always only wanted the best for him," but who embarked on a criminal career nevertheless, "although he always got everything he needed." The assumption seems reasonable that the aggressiveness of this youth is a result of the oversating of his minimum factors; he escapes into a life of crime for want of knowing how else to cope.

A primary concern in communicational marketing, therefore, is the accurate identification of needs generated by a supply shortage. Missing this mark in advertising messages creates paradoxes for those being addressed—paradoxes in which the targeted audience members feel under attack and against which they feel impelled to defend themselves.

Here the danger is not only one of failing to reach the recipient with a purely pragmatic, psychological advertising message; there is also the danger of putting oneself in the position of an *enemy*.

An important role with respect to these mechanisms is played by the social context in which the communication pattern occurs. From the perspective of vacationers from northern Europe, southern European countries, such as Spain, France, Italy, Turkey, or Greece, are viewed as being particularly hospitable. One also speaks of an "exaggerated hospitality." It is a little bit puzzling how such a positive characteristic as hospitality can be viewed as exaggerated and hence as somewhat negative. The reason this striking character trait predominates in certain countries is not because better people live there but rather because of the high value placed by society on hospitality as a personal virtue. Hospitality—that is, taking care of the welfare of guests—ranks close to the top of the cultural hierarchy of values.

If you have ever been a guest of an Italian or French family, then you know the traditional communication patterns at meals, for example. The guest is given the feeling by all present of being the absolute center of interest; on such an evening, everything revolves around the guest. The hosts make it clear to the guest that they will spare no effort to ensure his or her complete satisfaction and well-being.

But at some point even the hungriest tourist has eaten to the full. Not even the most exquisite enticements can induce him or her to accept further hospitality. For the guest, the most hospitable thing the hosts could do now would be to leave him or her alone. He or she is in the position of having to request a new form of hospitality from the host, namely to refrain from being hospitable, thereby exhibiting a perfect double-bind paradox. It is now up to the guest to redefine the proffered hospitality, creating an interactive dilemma. However, the host sees his task as that of taking care of his guest. And now he is supposed to care for his guest by not taking care of him? In accordance with the principle of searching for order in paradoxical situations, the host will ask his guest, "Didn't you like the meal?"

The cause of this double bind lies in the opposing views held by the two cultures. On the one side, "Northern Europeans aren't particularly hospitable, for if you say you're full they immediately accept the statement at face value and don't make certain that you really don't still want something." And on the other side, "Southern Europeans are overly hospitable because they simply don't want to accept the fact that one has had enough!"

If you now ask how needs can be created, then the answer is simple here as well. Forget it! Needs cannot be produced. They exist or they don't exist, or they don't exist yet. The attempt to generate needs with advertising statements amounts to telling consumers what they want or what they ought to want. Such attempts will meet with resistance.

Communicational marketing identifies existing needs by looking for minimum factors in the complex organism of the market and then supplying them. If you manage to identify minimum factors that, ideally, you alone can provide with your product, you have already almost won right there. The aim of a product manager shouldn't consist in creating new needs but in finding signs of already existing deficiencies in minimum factors. These situations signal supply shortages. If your product offers a solution at this point, it will most definitely meet with the highest degree of market acceptance.

Put this to the test. Analyze a small but carefully targeted group of customers, perhaps by making a survey, and find out within a given area what the most important thing is for them at the moment. If you can offer this target group a solution for precisely the problem described, they will go to you for the product in question. For *you* are clearly the one in a position to satisfy what is perhaps their most important need at the present time.

Security and Stability of Order

It can safely be assumed that offering someone something always creates a conflict situation with potentially paradoxical features. The person is compelled to make a decision in any event, even if the decision consists simply in turning away.

We recall how human beings react in conflict situations. Three reactions can be observed.

1. The person gets onto the same communicational level and reacts with a *counterparadox*. This response doesn't save the situation but does do some justice to it.
2. The pressure of a paradox is avoided by *not* communicating, by refusing to communicate in digital form. Although it is impossible not to communicate, the refusal will at least prevent a continued involvement and a possible escalation of the situation. However, the problem with this response is that the one who refuses to communicate always appears to be the loser. The refusal to communicate is interpreted as an inability to do so.
3. The third reaction consists in the search for a plausible new order or frame of reference—one that seems to offer the only way out of the dilemma. Only within this new order, or so it seems, do solutions become possible again. By this means, a person confronted with a decision can find the *assurance and security* of being able to justify their decisions to themselves and to others. The manifestation of the respective personality in such communicational frames of reference provides the person concerned with a sense of stability and hence of security.

Communicational Defense

Advertising atacks

Filter and rejection:
kick it out of the system

COMMUNICATIONAL MARKETING

Suggestive messages are always in danger of being blocked off as blatant attempts at manipulation.

Considering its intercommunicative origin, the desire for a certain degree of stability and continuity can perhaps be designated as the most fundamental need, and the most relevant one for marketing. Security and stability should not be understood here as representing an ultraconservative standpoint based on the uncompromising preservation of "tried and true" patterns and structures (although this political, sociological, and ideological phenomenon could have the same communicational origin). The need for security described here has to be understood on a more individual basis. A restless person, for example, a person intent on constant change, has found the appropriate form of order and stability in this particular lifestyle.

An advertising message that puts in question these manifestations of order cannot be accepted by the recipient. This state of affairs is reflected by behavioral reactions to fashion trends. A fashion trend—longer hair, ragged jeans, or the cell phone carried by the mobile businessperson—can succeed for a short time in circumventing the ordering mechanisms of communication, or in replacing them by means of a high degree of social pressure. But as soon as it becomes evident that these trends only offer illusory solutions, then the search for a new order, or the call for the old order, starts up once again. For the desire for security and dependability cannot be satisfied in the long run by shifting trends in fashion.

If is not a question of quick money but rather one of discriminating, far-sighted marketing, then the consideration of these principles of order plays a large role.

Chapter 18
Too Much Is Too Much

The Problem Is Communication

Of course! Every entrepreneur, every engineer, and everyone else who wants to sell something (or someone) thinks that their product or performance is good or better than those of others. Psychological marketing frequently even postulates this assumption as a prerequisite for success, in accordance with the motto "Believe in yourself (or in your product) and you will be successful."

The positive roll of healthy self-confidence, particularly in the development of individual personality, is not being disputed here. Experienced psychologists offer a number of very promising methods for the effective influencing of individual self-confidence.

But in communicational marketing completely different mechanisms are also at work. Communicational marketing as it is postulated here goes far beyond the intraspecific laws of individual psychology by taking communication channels into consideration, as well as their influence on decision-making.

Whoever wants to have success with advertising today must make contact with reality as quickly as possible. But the only reality that plays a role here is to be found in the heads of those to whom something is to be sold.

It is not the intention of communicational marketing to create something new or unique. Rather it makes use of thought patterns long since established in communicational rules, transforms them, and links them together in new associations for a realistic marketing approach.

Today, the consumer market hardly responds at all to psychological marketing, apart from short-lived phenomena in various fashion trends. The advertising landscape is just simply too saturated by an immense flood of well thought out psychological strategies offering more and more products from more and more companies with more and more intensive advertising ballyhoo.

What is called for is a changeover to a strategy based on communication. We live today in a communication flood that is getting worse by the day. The per capita consumption of advertising is steadily increasing. In 1950, U.S. advertisers spent $171 million, or 3% of the total advertising volume, on TV advertising. By 2004, spending jumped to nearly $68 *billion*, and accounted for more than 25% of all U.S ad spending.[16]

It is hard to understand how in such a communicationally polluted society an enthusiastic advertising strategist could still speak of the "high impact" of an individual advertising initiative. Every agency and every company that engages in any form of advertising must realize that, however clever or sophisticated their ad work is, in view of the vastness of the market they can only make a tiny impression in the total bombardment that rains down on the consumer day after day.

I am therefore convinced that the present monster advertising budgets—especially for television commercials—will be sharply cut back in the next few years for the simple reason that advertising effects will hardly be obtainable anymore. Advertising gets on people's nerves. It is getting to be too much. There is no movie, no sporting event that gets broadcast by private television organizations these days without entire blocks of commercials. The TV networks compound the impertinence of these annoyances even further by turning up the volume during the advertising blocks—with the result that the tormented viewer quickly reaches for the remote control to change channels or press the mute button.

Regardless of how enormous the budget, an advertising campaign can hardly have the effect of a bulldozer that rolls over an entire market in one fell swoop, as it were. A single advertising initiative is more like a little clear space that opens up briefly in the all-engulfing communication fog—a fog which, if the figures are to be believed, gets denser by the day.

In this confusing jungle, you only have a chance of being noticed at all if you know the ground rules of communication, focus on clearly limited objectives, and concentrate your resources on a particular segment or niche. Put briefly, the key to success is communicational marketing.

As we have seen, the brain is able to protect itself against too much information as well as against paradoxical communication. Human beings can block out signals in the context of intercommunication; they can simply reject a large part of the offered information that does not fit into their

---

[16]   "U.S. Ad Spending Totals by Media," 2006 Fact Pack, *Advertising Age.*

preferred patterns. The human brain seems to assimilate what can be fitted into earlier experiences, i.e., what corresponds to its ordering principles.

This characteristic is probably essential for human survival. For if people did not have the ability to filter information they would have to react to every suggestion, every offer, and every stimulus. Imagine trying to stroll unscathed through an urban shopping arcade in such an unprotected state, reacting to every influence. The absence of these protective mechanisms would probably trigger an insane spending spree, which is known to be a pathological phenomenon.

Millions of dollars are wasted in the attempt to change worldviews and frames of reference by means of advertising. The pointlessness of this aim can easily be demonstrated by taking the example of having a simple opinion on a trivial subject.

Let us consider for a moment the characteristics of having an opinion in the very subjective area of fashion. It is quite conceivable that somebody likes red patent-leather shoes. A critical observer could say, "This isn't an opinion in the first place and surely not part of a frame of reference or a worldview; it is just a matter of taste." From the communicational perspective, however, in this person's frame of reference red patent-leather shoes rank high in the category "shoes." It would hardly be possible, even with psychological means, to topple them from this position—for everything that raises doubts about this frame of reference is immediately countered by communicational defense mechanisms that are automatically triggered. You have certainly experienced the way people feel personally attacked in discussions when the "opponent" has, in fact, merely presented a factual argument against their point of view. Everyone is familiar with the feeling of being attacked if their views are put into question, even by persons with whom they have never been in contact.

Once someone has formed and categorized an "opinion" in her personal frame of reference, it is very difficult to persuade her to give it up again. And advertising with its pitch "This is so terrific you've got to buy it!" is the worst conceivable means.

"I already know what I think." This is the attitude that most people have, despite enthusiastic public propagation of tolerance for other views. At present, this pseudotolerant stance is enjoying renewed popularity: "Of course, I am always glad to let myself be convinced by another point of view!" Here the emphasis lies on "convince"—meaning "This really will take some convincing."

However, if people are told something about which they know little or nothing, quite different behavior is exhibited toward assertions made by others. The audience ratings for newscasts and weather forecasts are higher and more consistent than for any other television broadcast. When it is a question of experiencing or learning something, or developing oneself further, even the most pronounced frames of reference seem to be more open; they allow new information to incorporate itself into the "gaps," as it were.

On the other hand, the head-on attempt to *change* the consciousness of the consumer with psychological means can lead to catastrophic results in marketing.

The compact disc, as a conventional, reasonably priced data carrier, has revolutionized the possibilities of electronic data processing (EDP). And the DVD, which can hold more than six times the data of a CD, has further reduced the number of storage units needed to contain a set of information. There are hardly any catalogs, lists, phone books, recipes, or even complete legal data bases that are not offered on CDs or DVDs. Thus, at an affordable price, private computer users can build up a multifunctional data base at home that leaves hardly any questions unanswered. In order to completely assimilate all this data, however, the owner of such a collection would have to live several lives. And the present-day possibilities of EDP are even more fantastic. The Internet extends this information flood practically to infinity. But who is working on a gigabyte memory capacity for your brain? Who is helping consumers to orient themselves in this totally overloaded complexity, which continues to get more and more overwhelming?

It is not the products that constitute the problem in modern marketing. Nor is the problem the demand for better and better quality at lower and lower prices. The problem is communication itself.

Simple Advertising Statements = Higher Quality of Communication

If your advertising message is to have even the slightest chance of being noticed at all, then the only semantic means to this end is *simplification*. This requisite is by no means intended to cast doubt on the intelligence of consumers. On the contrary. As stated at the outset, one of the main premises of communicational marketing is the ascription of the highest degree of communicative competence to the consumer.

But the simpler the message is formulated, the less the transmitter runs the risk of entangling the recipient in confusion. In communicational marketing less means more. Every statement should be checked again and again for ambiguities at the relational level. The message should formulate only those contents that have a realistic chance of being integrated into an existing frame of reference. Everything else is a waste of money. One of the main bottlenecks is created by the quantity of communication trying to access the various individual frames of reference. This makes a higher quality of communication an absolute necessity. However, you won't find this quality in the products themselves or in sensationally low prices. What is meant here is rather the manner of communicating.

If a problem arises, everyone tends automatically to look for solutions in their own perception of things. A solution is normally to be found here for marketing issues as well. If this approach fails, there is a real danger of looking to the product for solutions. But this way, which might well be the right course of action with respect to many traditional matters of decision, is completely wrong in marketing. For here the solution lies with the consumer alone.

Since only fractions of advertising messages can ever reach a person's frame of reference at all, the only thing that counts in advertising statements is the way the recipient reacts to them. Psychological marketing analyzes the question "What does the customer want?" Communicational marketing goes a decisive step further. Here the question is "How does the customer react to the message?"

The truth as your customer sees it is the only truth that counts. In comparison with this, the qualities of the product are irrelevant—for when they are defined by the transmitter, all they ultimately reflect is the truth of the transmitter.

Corporations in the Western industrial nations have turned communication into an economically relevant factor, and the East is now adding massively to the trend. And as is often the case in free enterprise systems, resources that are apparently inexhaustible are squandered with abandon. This way of dealing with great capacities always leads to social problems. Instrumentalizing communication to help cope with economic and social problems becomes a further problem. This problem is conspicuous in the constipation of communication channels, which reduces to a trickle the amount of information that gets through.

And what does get through has an increasingly questionable moral quality, as is manifested by the increased propensity for violence on the part of children. As a result of the constant exposure to violence, children no longer filter out the ever more spectacular and brutal aspects from the communication flood. Instead, they apparently actively seek out just these aspects. Violence is becoming a standard item in the general frame of reference and hence will at some point become the basis for dealing with conflicts—a highly disturbing social development.

Consider the following statistics about media saturation.

- In 2005, about 172,000 new books were published in the United States alone. A single person would have read around the clock for more than ninety-seven years to cope with the production of just one year.[17]

---

[17]   http://www.bowker.com/press/bowker/2006_0509_bowker.htm

- One of the most frequently used media in the U.S is television—98.9% of all U.S. households have at least one color television set
- The average U.S. family has the TV on for more than seven hours per day (more than forty-nine hours per week). The television picture is produced by a succession of individual images (twenty-five per second). This means, even if it is not registered consciously, that the average American family is confronted with approximately 750,000 television images per day.[18]
- In 2005, almost thirteen million metric tons of newsprint is produced for North American newspapers.[19] This means that on average almost 87 kilograms of newsprint is consumed per capita per year. Faced with this flood of information, what percentage can individuals actually take in?

Almost four hundred words of text are printed on a 17-ounce packet of a particular brand of oatmeal. If you requested the offered booklet with twenty-one recipes, you could occupy yourself with this product for an entire weekend. The leaflet accompanying one brand of simple cough syrup consists of 1,980 words. If you buy the latest high-tech VCR, you could be busy for up to a whole day reading the instructions.

The German Bundestag passes approximately five hundred laws per annum. This could provide at least one week of reading material and an additional fourteen days for understanding what one has read. In the same time period, government agencies, regional authorities, internal revenue offices, etc. release thousands of new regulations, amendments, settlements— and this in a jargon guaranteed to stifle even the most burning enthusiasm for language.

Does all that hold any interest for you? Look back at the great events in world history. It has certainly not been the long, expansive speeches and reports steeped in self-glorification that have had an impact and taken root in people's frames of reference. On the contrary, simple, short, and concise communications are what make a lasting impression. The Ten Commandments of the Old Testament, with its "laughable" 297 words, is one of the best examples. The Lord's Prayer comprises about sixty words; the U.S. Declaration of Independence consists of three hundred words.

A recently effected ordinance of the ministers of the European Union for the determination of new norms for imported bananas contains 24,711 words.

---

[18] http://209.85.165.104/search?q=cache:DLPq8npObnkJ:www.tvturnoff.org/images/facts%26figs/factsheets/FactsFigs.pdf+average+U.S.+tv+per+day&hl=en&ct=clnk&cd=1&gl=us

[19] http://www.newsandtech.com/issues/2006/04-06/nt/04-06_newsprint.htm

(It could also have been 24,715 words, but that would make no difference; it wouldn't make the matter any more interesting or important.)

Our mental track has ended in a traffic jam. A questionnaire prior to the U.S. presidential election in 1988 tried to determine what the average American citizen knew about George H. W. Bush. Most people recalled three attributes: He was good-looking. He came from Texas. He was the vice president of the United States. As you know, this average amount of information was enough to get Bush elected president of the United States in 1988. But there were, in fact, a number of Americans who didn't know even that much about Bush. A concurrent survey conducted in supermarkets by *People* magazine revealed that 44% of the readers interviewed had no idea at all who George Bush was, although at that time he had already been vice president for four years.

On the other hand, 93% of the customers surveyed knew Mr. Clean, the figure on Procter & Gamble's cleaning fluid bottle. The consumers interviewed recognized Mr. Clean despite the fact that he had disappeared from television screens in the United States ten years before.

This illustrates the power of communicational marketing if simple advertising statements are conveyed and people's frames of reference are taken into account.

In a communication-saturated society, communication becomes extremely difficult. It can in fact be preferable to desist from communication altogether—or at least until it is absolutely clear what frame of reference should be addressed.

One should be aware of the fact (coincidentally stated by former basketball star Charles Barkley in the ads for Right Guard deodorants) that there is never a second chance to make the first impression! There is only one answer to the problem of the communication flood in our society: communicational marketing. This involves getting away from product glorification and technological jargon in advertising statements and boiling the message down to a very clear, short statement instead. A new way of thinking for a new era.

World Media Champions

In contrast to the United States, Germany still had only three national television stations (the local stations normally did not broadcast any commercials) up until a few years ago. Now there are more than forty commercial channels on the German television market. To these must be added all the foreign television channels that can be received with satellite dishes.

Things aren't that simple in the United States. We are world champions in the construction of newer and newer systems and mechanisms for transmitting ever more material. You can use all kinds of television media—commercial television, cable TV, satellite television, public television—and all this can, of course, be supplemented with videos. In addition, local radio broadcasts send the latest news and information from every locality. In every town, one is confronted with posters and billboards as well—not to forget all the newspapers and magazines, morning editions, evening papers, dailies, weeklies, Sunday editions, hobbyist magazines, economics journals, professional journals, etc. Nor can you fail to miss advertising on buses, trucks, streetcars, subways, and taxicabs.

For the foreseeable future, there is no end to the advertising avalanche in sight. However, it can hardly be assumed that the product-information level of the consumer has increased proportionally to this proliferation. One is confronted with more and more advertising but the human brain is nevertheless incapable of a greater degree of assimilation. The receptivity of the human brain is limited.

Although the financial potential for even more advertising is certainly available, it seems doubtful that the assimilation capacity of the consumer can keep pace. Thousands of advertising messages compete every single day for a tiny share of the consumer's attention. The battlefield is the communicational frame of reference of the consumer.

Is it any wonder that advertising is a constant subject of criticism for consumers? Market researchers have found that consumers actually boycotts products whose advertising they find annoying. These same researchers have also found out that the consumers find advertising less and less entertaining and useful.[20] In addition, activists are mobilizing highly coordinated campaigns urging consumers via SMS messaging to boycott specific products.[21]

Advertising is a cutthroat business in which every mistake comes at a high price. Communicational marketing, the practice of taking into consideration communicational mechanisms, should help to avoid these mistakes.

World Production Champions

Let us consider all the new products and services developed daily to satisfy the demand of our industrial societies, taking the United States as an example.

The average supermarket in the United States offers three times as many brands as it did in 1991. (Source: http://www.wired.com/wired/archive/12.11/brands.html) We are now able to choose from three hundred types of spaghetti,

---

[20]   1996 study by Germany's Society for Consumer, Market, and Sales Research
[21]   http://www.textually.org/textually/archives/2003/03/000134.htm

for example, instead of from a mere forty types. The packaging industry is expanding its capacities to accommodate further increases.

Scientists who have conducted experiments on the efficiency of the human brain are familiar with the phenomenon of "stimuli flooding." The assimilation capacity of the human brain is quite apparently limited. If a certain limit is exceeded, the brain simply switches off. Dentists have conducted experiments on the basis of these discoveries, placing headphones on patients and increasing the volume to a point where there was scarcely any sensation of pain in the tooth.

In order to better understand the nature of our communications, we shall now take a closer look at the end point of every communication: the human brain. Put simply, the brain has a special "drawer," like the database of a computer, for all information that is to be saved. This is why the brain is frequently compared to a computer. With regard to the memory processes, this comparison seems plausible. But there is a fundamental difference. The computer has to accept every type of input provided that it conforms to certain digital semantics. The brain (of a healthy person), on the other hand, does not have to accept anything or anyone, even if the same language is spoken.

On the contrary, the human brain rejects all information that cannot be processed. It accepts only such new information as can be squared with its present mind-set, its present ordering principles. All other information is invariably blocked out, or at least withdrawn from immediate consciousness.

Take two abstract drawings. Write the name "Miller" on one of them and the name "Degas" on the other. Then ask a friend what he thinks of the two sketches. If he likes the drawing by the painter named Miller, make him the following proposal: he may keep one of the two pictures under the condition that he doesn't sell it. Now then, which one is he going to choose?

Pour a bottle of cheap wine in an empty, fifty-year-old Burgundy bottle. Now pour some of it reverently into the glass of a would-be wine connoisseur and ask for an opinion.

If buying decisions were made exclusively at the rational level, advertising would cease to have a function. If advertising took place exclusively at the informational level—that is, if relational aspects did not exist—then companies could save a lot of money. Advertising would then be pointless. It would suffice simply to describe the products, whereupon consumers would decide on the basis of matter-of-fact considerations whether they needed them or whether they could do without them.

Harvard psychologist Dr. George A. Miller has found that the human brain cannot process more than seven items at a time.[22] The number seven

---

[22]   Miller, George A. "Living Systems." *Behavioral Science* 10 (1965).

appears in many kinds of contexts where something is supposed to be remembered: the Seven Wonders of the World, Seven Up, Snow White and the Seven Dwarfs, etc. When the attempt was made to list several brands in one product category, only seldom were more than seven brand names mentioned. Furthermore, even this holds true only if the interviewee has a strong interest in the product categories in question. In the case of products for which the interviewee showed little or no personal interest, the average number of brands indicated was only three.

According to a newspaper survey, eighty out of one hundred Germans can name only two members of the Bundestag, the lower house of the German parliament. If the intellectual storage capacity of human beings is too small to cope with such questions, how are consumers supposed to keep up with the constantly proliferating number of brand names? Thirty years ago American smokers had a choice of seventeen different brands offered by the six leading cigarette manufacturers. Today there are more than two hundred varieties on the market. Imagine the length of a cigarette machine for two hundred packets!

This fetish of product-line proliferation, which results from the diversification strategies dreamed up at our universities, has affected every branch of industry from cars through beer to computer systems. This has gone so far that by now total confusion obtains in some branches, e.g., the computer industry.

For years everyone has been talking about specialization, total quality, and the necessity of concentrating on market niches. But it seems as if these insights are too difficult to implement. Many attempts fizzle out after initial successes because they get bogged down in the old diversification patterns.

In order to reduce the immense complexity of the communication avalanche for their part, consumers are forced to simplify everything. The classification and reduction of people, products and brands to a necessary minimum is not a sign of superficiality or a lack of intelligence on the part of the consumer but is rather a natural reaction to existing pressure. The increase in superficiality and materialism among young people, which is so often lamented, is an understandable consequence of, and reaction to, the communication flood.

For the above reasons, communicational marketing is insistent about short and uncomplicated advertising statements. Marketers should forgo long explanations, elaborate product specifications, and declarations of intention. Only short and easy-to-remember statements have a chance of receiving any attention at all.

Chapter 19

The Product Ladder in the Frame of Reference

In order to cope with the explosion in the number of new products offered on the market without suffering adverse affects, we have learned to mentally categorize products and brands. The mind sets up product "ladders," to use an apt metaphor. Products belonging to one group are hierarchically arranged—like rungs—on these product ladders. Each individual rung is defined by a brand name. The number of the rungs on the ladders can vary considerably.

This model can be illustrated with the following example: For certain product groups, men and women construct quite different ladder formations in their respective frames of reference. Men often set up more ladders for technological products like cars, stereo equipment, or toy train sets. The ladders of female consumers sometimes contain more fashion, jewelry, or cosmetic items. This is not the hackneyed dichotomy one might think it is. On the contrary, in recent years there has been a shift in the areas of interest on both sides, as well as a certain leveling of the differences. The essential difference lies in the *number* of individual rungs on the respective product ladders.

Ask fifty women and fifty men at random to name all the car makes that occur to them. One can bet that the male test candidates will have constructed more rungs for the product "automobile." When it comes to the manufacturers of cosmetics the result will probably be just the opposite. If one concentrated the line of inquiry on subsections—e.g., "Name ten, or even five, lipstick manufacturers ..."—then the male test candidates would make a poor showing, the author included. If one asked the ladies to name three makes or types of car with twelve-cylinder engines, things would start to get critical for them as well. Now, I wouldn't want to wager a guess on the number of rungs, or brand names, on the respective fashion ladders; in this area, there has been a strong increase of interest on the part of male consumers in the last few years.

These systems of rungs and ladders constitute the *communicational frames of reference*. Of relevance is, of course, the relative position of the individual products on the rungs; these positions represent clear and distinct value judgments. The first three positions, which in these surveys are always named quickly and without a lot of reflection, obviously play the leading roles with respect to quality.

It is also worth noting that product classification does not necessarily have to reflect personal preference. This is evidenced by the fact that market trends or widely held opinions can occupy definite positions in frames of reference even if there is no individual interest in the respective category at all. Some manufacturers (Coke, Procter & Gamble, 3M, Colgate, Kleenex, Kodak, Xerox, etc.), have even managed to make their market position an element of general knowledge and to integrate themselves into people's frames of reference, as it were, without any particular demonstration of merit or without even necessarily a direct effort to do so. That's quite a remarkable marketing success.

Here is another example taken from direct interviews: Car makers have achieved particularly sharp profiles in this store of general knowledge. Ask an environmentalist bicycling along on a cold winter's day in wooden sandals wearing a hand-knitted natural-wool sweater and cap what in his opinion are the best known and most important automobile brands. After reproaching you for the outrageous presumption of asking him such a question in the first place, of associating him with cars in any form whatsoever, sooner or later this individual will overcome his inner resistance and hurl at you the brand names Mercedes, BMW, and Lexus. From this example, it can be inferred that some product ladders are not the result of individual construction but are simply assimilated or copied into existing systems without necessarily having to reflect individual preference.

According to the communicational understanding, whenever it is a question of raising the consumer's estimation of the value of a product relative to that of the competition, then the higher-ranking product first has to be displaced from its rung. For once a ladder (product segment) has been set up, there are no any empty rungs that can simply be had for the taking. This would involve the hopeless attempt of a frontal attack on the frame of reference and value system involved. Once certain positions have established themselves, the primary task is to defend them, for they constitute a part of one's individual identity.

Human beings are defined by what they think and feel. A natural instinct of survival impels one to fend off everything that could pose a threat to one's frame of reference or system of order. I would even go so far as to maintain that a brand that has succeeded in establishing itself in the frame of reference of a consumer can become a part of that consumer's identity. It makes no difference whether the product is lipstick (Maybelline), an automobile (Mercedes), a watch (Rolex), baby shampoo (Johnson & Johnson), a high-tech computer (Hewlett-Packard), or whatever. A person is what a person thinks. The basis of what a person thinks can be innate, learned, or imitated. It can also be just simply imagined; none of this makes any difference. Communicational marketing has found that the crystallization of thought patterns and the effects on situational behavior and individual perceptions are the result of communicational mechanisms.

The Product Ladder

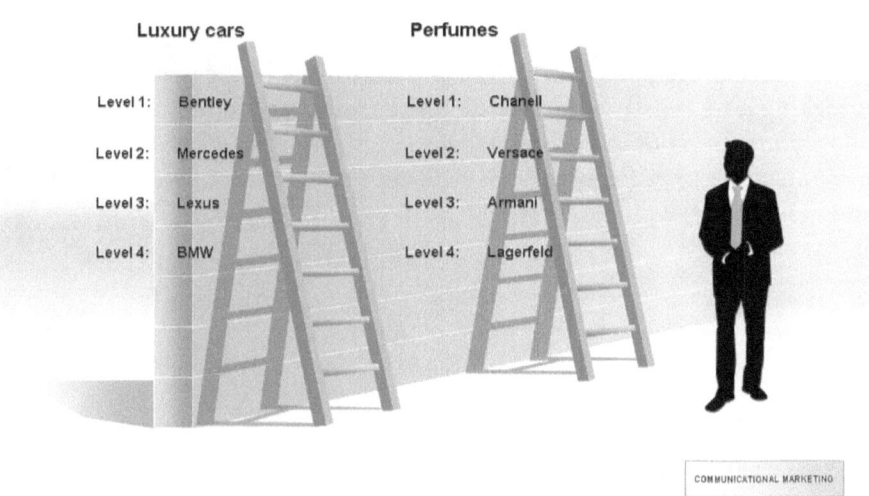

(These rankings are for illustrative purposes only and are not intended to reflect any actual state of affairs.)

The general impression one gets from Western markets is that many companies seem to base their advertising strategies on the premise that there is no competition at all. By so doing, the awareness and competence of consumers are ignored in an unpardonable manner. A great deal of advertising seems to take place in a vacuum. What an illusion! To be sure, under isolated, communicationally sterile laboratory conditions, models can be simulated from a psychological perspective that fly in the face of entire value systems. But other conditions and hence other laws obtain among the communication monsters out in the wilds.

A current example is the commercial by the company Hellmann, which produces mayonnaise (Hellmann's.) At present, the company is running a daily TV ad that, from a psychological perspective, is perfectly produced. There is good use of color and a catchy tune that phonetically builds up the brand name: "Hell, Hell, Hellmann."

From the communicational perspective, however, any success of this commercial (which might amount to a slight increase in sales due mainly to the high rate of repetition) can hardly justify the effort and expense. For Hellmann claims within one and the same commercial that "Hellmann's is new," and then a bit later, "Hellmann's is the most popular mayonnaise in the world!"

From the perspective of an attentive viewer, one must ask oneself, "How stupid does Hellmann really think the consumer is?" How can a mayonnaise be new and at the same time the most popular one in the world? Hellmann is making a reckless attempt to ride roughshod over the frames of reference of mayonnaise consumers. Even consumers with little knowledge of the mayonnaise market (who perhaps have not yet erected a ladder with Kraft and Heinz on it) will feel deceived.

A Communicational Approach: Extending the Frame of Reference

In view of all the defense mechanisms against "aggressors" that people build into their frames of reference, one can ask how a rung, even one of the lowest ranking ones, can become occupied at all. As already indicated, it is not the intention of this book to present easy answers in the style of some marketing and manager publications in line with the motto "If you do "a" then surely "b" will follow." Communicational marketing means, in this context, the integration of communicational factors into existing marketing strategies. The daily practice of business consulting shows that companies are putting ever greater budgets into ever more gigantic advertising projects only to complain ultimately about their low degree of effectiveness and appropriateness. The reason for this lies to an increasing extent in the fact that regardless of how impressive and imaginative the strategies are, they are not examined in terms of their communicational effect.

The Differentiated Product Ladder

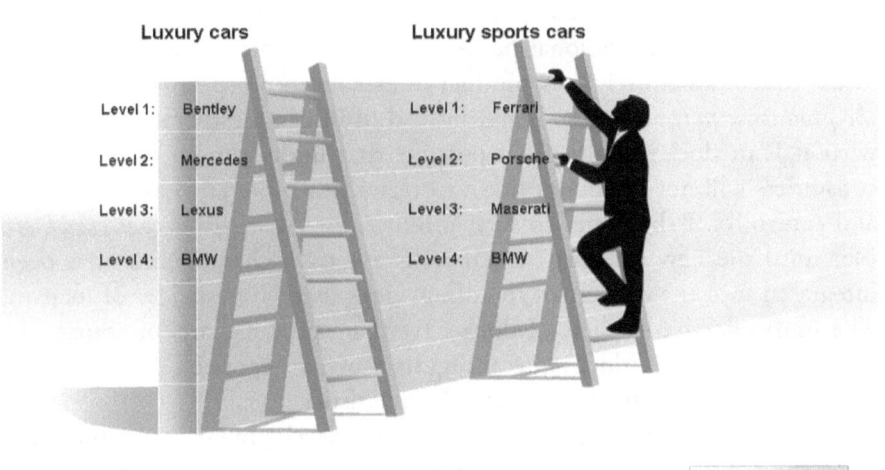

	Luxury cars		Luxury sports cars
Level 1:	Bentley	Level 1:	Ferrari
Level 2:	Mercedes	Level 2:	Porsche
Level 3:	Lexus	Level 3:	Maserati
Level 4:	BMW	Level 4:	BMW

COMMUNICATIONAL MARKETING

(These rankings are for illustrative purposes only and are not intended to reflect any actual state of affairs.)

Turning now to the question of a possible communicational approach, communicational marketing proposes to offer the market a new "ladder." This does not mean new products at all costs. On the contrary, not only do individual rungs on a ladder compete against each other; there is also competitive pressure among the various ladders making up the frame of reference as a whole. Since the brain does not have unlimited space for the accommodation of everything new, an active process of selection takes place.

The frame of reference is more receptive if it is presented with something that *can be related to already existing structures.* (Perhaps this offers a further explanation for the earlier assertion of the self-perpetuating character of these reference systems.) The reason for this is that all impressions (here, products and ideas) that can be related to prestructured reference areas—i.e., already existing ladders—*confirm and reinforce* their respective constellations.

This also explains why some products have proved to be total flops in spite of being absolutely unique or of addressing entirely new areas of life when they were launched. There were simply no referential structures in existence at the time to which the new product could be related in some way.

From a communicational point of view, therefore, it can be advisable in the case of an entirely new product to explain to prospective buyers *what the product is not,* or *does not have,* instead of informing them straight away what it is or does have, for it is possible that under certain circumstances consumers will not be in a position to relate this product to existing values and categories. I shall refer to such products as *"I-don't-have-that" products.* Not until the new category, which lacks a certain characteristic, has been integrated into the context of the others does it receive a ladder of its own. The most effective of these "I-don't-have-that" products are, of course, the *first* ones to set up a ladder representing their own category on the strength of the conspicuous *absence* of a certain characteristic.

Let us take as an example an interesting development in the food and beverages sector. With many consumers, food and beverages enjoy a position of relatively high priority as an expression of prosperity and luxury. In any case, they constitute for most people the subject matter of daily consumer questions. A number of manufacturers in this sector have succeeded in positioning completely "new" derivative products on this market by emphasizing what their products did *not* have.

Think back for a moment. Do you recall how all that got started? It all began with *sugar-free* carbonated soft drinks, *low-fat* butter, cottage cheese with *almost no* calories, cola *without* caffeine. The effect of these "without" or "I-don't-have-that" products was enormous. A soft drink without sugar was indeed a totally new product. But since carbonated soft drinks already existed, sugar-free soft drinks quickly gained access to the prevailing frame of reference in spite of their newness. And the fact that they did not possess a certain characteristic—i.e., sugar (a negative for many weight-watchers)— made them highly interesting as well.

It wasn't until some time later that these products got christened with the appellation "lite." By now, lite products most definitely have a ladder of their own. But without the prior development of the concept of products lacking a certain characteristic ("I-don't-have-that" products), the concept "lite" probably would not have been so readily accepted as a new "category." It will be recalled that the first motorcycle was called a bicycle with an auxiliary engine (*without* pedals), and the first car was called the "*horseless* carriage."

In today's market, the ranking of the competition within consumers' frame of reference is just as important as the ranking of one's own company or product—sometimes even more so.

The often cited Avis campaign is a telling example of a successful competitive strategy. In the case of Avis, what was decisive in the minds of consumers was the way the company defined its own rank vis-à-vis the market leader. The wording of the advertisement was as follows: "Avis is number two among rental cars. So why drive with us? Because we try harder!"

For a number of years in succession, the rental car agency had big losses. Then, after the company admitted it was number two, it started to make appreciable profits. Avis began making money simply by accepting the existing ranking of Hertz rather than trying to attack the consumers' frame of reference head-on with disregard and denials.

One understands the success of the Avis program better if one takes a look into the heads of potential customers and imagines a product ladder there with the label "rental car." All the rungs on the product ladder are labeled with brand names. The name Hertz occupies first place. The name Avis is in second place.

Some psychologically oriented marketing strategists explained the Avis success differently. From a psychological perspective, one could be tempted to think the success of Avis was due to the fact that Avis *suggested* to customers that they "try harder" and are therefore more reliable and more reasonably priced. But putting out more effort is hardly the decisive formula for success in marketing.

One possibility of communicational marketing consists in "creeping up" on an already existing ladder in the consumer's reference system. Almost two out of every three soft drinks consumed in the United States are cola beverages. By connecting its product with one already well known to consumers, 7UP was able to establish the "non-cola position" as an alternative to cola beverages. One can visualize the three rungs of the cola ladder in the United States as follows:

1: Coca-Cola
2: Pepsi
3: 7UP

In order to find a unique, unmistakable place in consumer reference systems, you have to lay aside classical, objectifying logic, which is propounded in universities with such great élan. For classical logic stipulates that one has to find a conception either in oneself or in the product. In communicational marketing, however, this thinking is false. You have to look for your conception in the frames of reference and worldviews of *consumers*.

Chapter 20
Facts, Facts, Facts

The German news magazine *Focus*, which has only been established for a few years, has had to try to hold its own against the longstanding news magazine *der Spiegel*. The successes of *Focus* in terms of copies sold and advertising accounts, supported by the resources of a financially strong and highly committed publishing house (Burda), are easily comparable with those of *der Spiegel*. On the Internet, *Focus* rapidly became market leader in some areas due to its early involvement in this medium.

Focus succeeded in establishing itself in a relatively short period of time as number two among the influential political magazines in Germany. Previously, there had only been *der Spiegel*. After that nothing else followed for a long time. (Possibly *Stern* can be put in this category, but *Stern* lacked *der Spiegel's* image of a news magazine. *Stern* is more a competitor of *Bunte* since both of them offer mostly entertainment topics in addition to political information.)

This is a very respectable result for *Focus* in view of the completely oversaturated newspaper and magazine market. How did the magazine achieve such success?

Der Spiegel is number one in the area of political reporting. Because of its investigative journalism and aggressive documentation, *der Spiegel* enjoys an extremely widespread reputation. But despite the fact that the politicians of all parties fear *der Spiegel* on account of its "impertinence" and uncompromising stance, it is nevertheless regarded as a left-wing publication. To the right of *der Spiegel* were a number of news magazines, but no adequate ones. *Focus* hit on the idea of how to occupy this open position. Although no political side was spared by *Focus* either, the suggestion of an alternative to an existing product was alone sufficient to arouse the necessary interest—precisely by virtue of a "non-position." *Focus* won a large part of this battle just exactly not by communicating the message "We are a conservative news magazine!" Who cared whether or not there were any available niches for a conservative news magazine? What *Focus* did was to define itself as a "*non-left-wing*" news magazine. Bull's-eye!

The Highest Court: The Truth of the Consumer

Communicational marketing takes into account the subjective perceptions of the consumer. Particularly in quality management, there is increasing enthusiasm for the notion that marketing is a battle among *products*. Many companies believe that in the long run the best products—i.e., the highest quality or most functional ones—will win out in the end. Especially today, when more and more discounters are flooding the markets with bargain-basement prices and junk goods, the decision-makers of the big brand-name manufacturers are going on the defensive and excusing their declining sales with the statement "In the long run, our quality will beat the competition." The only question is *when*?

In modern marketing, "facts" are collected by all parties with stakes in the game. Every psychologically derived behavioral hypothesis is thoroughly checked and "verified" by means of elaborate statistical games and colored charts. Armed with this material, which usually is self-confirming, companies launch a frontal campaign against the consumer with the conviction that quality means power.

Despite the fact that this method of product glorification seems to be the most obvious and simple one, it is pure self-deception nonetheless. An objective, universally valid, all-encompassing reality does not exist! Even so-called facts are the result of subjective perceptions. No "best products" can be defined in this way, and most certainly not by those who produce them.

In communicational marketing, the only relevant factor for advertising messages that really exists consists in the perceptions—i.e., the frames of reference—of those being addressed. These are the only "facts" that count.

Almost all philosophers have propounded the relativity of truth in their life works. In modern marketing, however, one still seems to be convinced of being able to produce truths with large budgets. This is absurd.

The Objective Truth in Marketing

People employ any number of means to find their own personal truth, their mental scheme of things. In this process, the outside world plays a decisive role. Most people seem to have a natural impulse to project their views and way of life onto their surroundings. One reason for this behavior lies in the elemental need to communicate. This need to communicate arises in turn from the search for confirmation.

You are familiar with the situation in which you felt the need to tell something to someone, perhaps an experience that moved you deeply, or horrified you a great deal—especially if something has happened to you, an accident or a delightful, positive experience. However, you also will recall what a paralyzing feeling of disappointment comes over you when the person to whom you are euphorically relating your experience reacts with the tired remark "Yeah, I know all about that." The disillusionment can become total if this comment is then followed promptly by the remark "That's happened to me, too. But let me tell you something else that happened to me recently. It was much worse (or more beautiful) than that."

People look for confirmation in communication. They find it in newspapers, books, movies, television programs, magazines, and journals. They join clubs, organizations, political parties, sects, and other institutions; or they start a family in order to find confirmation and a sense of identity there. The external appearances and frameworks that people create for themselves define their view of the world. People often run the risk of relying on externalities as an evaluative instrument or control mechanism for their "own" thoughts.

In the case of a mentally ill person, this *can* go to such an extreme that the external world is understood as the sole reality. Such individuals thereby reduce their sense of self and create real problems for themselves. Some psychologically oriented marketing strategists seem to assume that this is the mind-set of the recipients of their advertising messages, meaning, in effect, that they consider their customers to be incompetent, mentally unstable, and pathological.

The reality of a "healthy," competent person is just the opposite. If a person's communicational protective mechanisms are functioning, the only reality of which they can be certain consists in their individual perception "I know what I see, think, and feel!" Such is the reality with which communicational marketing is concerned.

Marketing constitutes the attempt to influence the (many) perceptions that a person has. The attempt to influence these perceptions by means of intercontinental psychological warfare among products is doomed to fail. The rules of communicational marketing described here result from exactly the opposite point of view.

Communicational Perception

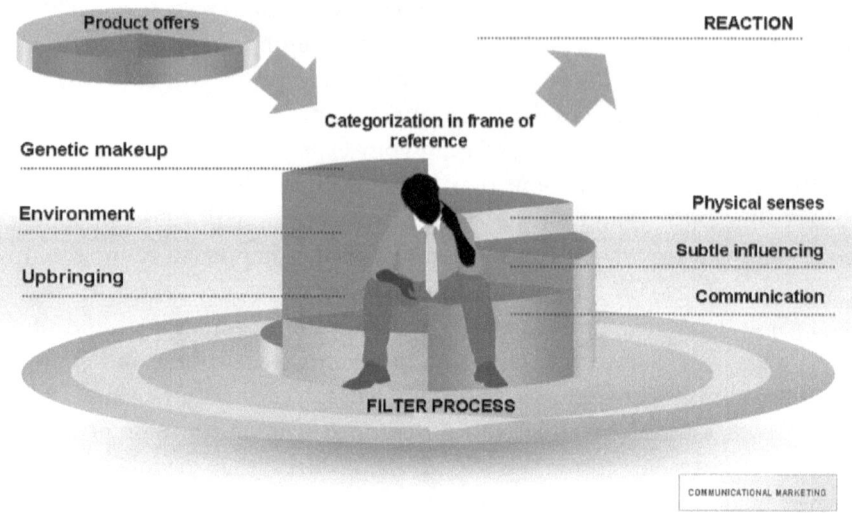

It is still a widespread assumption that the products themselves, their qualities and functions, are the flagships in the marketing war. From this premise, the conclusion is drawn that the focus of the marketing strategy should be on the product. This reasoning is deceptive, for it is only seemingly logical.

In the foregoing, you have already become acquainted with some of the ways in which, from the communicational perspective, perceptions arise. These insights hold the keys for making an impression on them.

Chapter 21
The Analytical Function of the Relational Level

If "truths" are postulated by specialists or experts, they seem more credible. If a question needs answering, one looks to an apparently competent expert for the answers. This way of finding out and verifying the truth about something generally works quite well in such areas as technology, medical research, the natural sciences, etc. We put our faith in an auto mechanic, a doctor, or a biologist when he or she tells us something in his or her area of competence.

Many advertising strategists avail themselves of this initial vote of confidence with *implied or suggested competence*. In commercials for toothpaste, cough drops, denture cleaner, and so forth, "competent doctors" or "experienced dentists" recommend the products being advertised. From a psychological perspective, the following is supposed to be suggested. If a doctor recommends the product, then there must be something to it; after all, one trusts one's own doctor. From the perspective of advertising psychology, this is apparently a consistent and logical strategy. But only apparently!

Again, the relational aspects of the message are woefully neglected here. In a five-to-ten-second commercial, it is by no means possible to simulate the atmosphere of a personal consultation with a doctor. It is presumptuous to assume that the consumer is naive enough to believe that competent doctors are involved at all. And even if the somewhat "naive" viewer does "believe" that the actors are, in fact, doctors, the impression will still be in the back of his mind that the doctor is being paid for his statement, and paid statements are anything but credible. Dr. Best (a real dentist), who glowingly recommends toothbrushes with rotating heads in his TV ads, does not constitute an exception.

The culmination of this psychological "insinuated competence" strategy was created by the English company Carter Wallace. Here the product, Pearly White (a tooth whitener), is not recommended by a dentist but—in all earnestness—by the *wife* of a dentist! Are you familiar with the job title *dentist's wife*? You aren't? Then watch more advertising, you can learn something!

Such psychological escapades in advertising bring the mechanism of the CIP Pyramid into play. If one does not want to suppose that Pearly White simply intended to occasion a little general amusement, but rather had the real intention of creating trust in the effectiveness of their products, then we have a prime example of how the intention gets transformed into the opposite in the CIP Pyramid: complete skepticism!

From the communicational standpoint, the frequently employed stratagem of using convincing role players to insinuate confidence in the effectiveness and functionality—or just simply the "truth"—of an advertising statement is a device best enjoyed with caution. Even if one's own presentation doesn't turns out quite as blatant and transparent as this commercial for tooth whitener, *the analytical function of the relational level* cannot be ignored with impunity.

Ferrero is one of the world's leading manufacturers of candy and cookies—the consumption of which can, of course, lead to obesity and tooth decay. The company thus has a problem in common with all food producers that use processed sugar: everyone knows that sugar, at least the excessive consumption of it, is harmful. Nevertheless, almost all chocolate and candy bar manufacturers try to convey through their advertising that their products are not only harmless but even healthy! (Chocolate for sports, chocolate for young people, the low-calorie candy bar, the healthy breakfast snack, etc.) Why in the world should consumers swallow the story that products containing sugar are healthy?

Confronted with this question, Ferrero called to mind the psychological effect of the good old conventional mother role. "A mother wouldn't give her children anything that wasn't good for them." This stereotype was imputed to be part of the standard mental furniture of viewers. Starting from this assumption, the commercial then states, "My mother always used to give *me* kids' chocolate ... a lot of milk, a little chocolate ... an extra portion of milk..."

Here, as well, roles and functions cloaked with a certain competence and expertise are used to infuse the advertisement with the desired aura of objectivity. In this case, the role employed is the classic one of the constantly concerned mother. Although here the *feigned competence*, as I would like to call it, is not so blatant as in the case of the "dentist's wife," the effect of the analytical function of the relational level is no different in this form of communication. The strategy of feigned competence may indeed still work well with children; children have a strong tendency to imitate roles. This simply reflects the fact that their inner frames of reference are not yet so well defined. This is also a reason why one can, in fact, speak of manipulative and thus harmful and ethically dubious aspects of advertising with respect to children.

Communicational marketing, on the other hand, assumes the existence of competent, mature, and paranoia-free consumers who are quite capable of taking note of the various aspects of the relational level of communication, differentiating among these, and then of judging and acting accordingly.

The strategy of feigned competence seems to be a very popular psychological instrument. A rather grotesque form of this strategy is the attempt to give products some semblance of a scientific character or foundation by dreaming up highly imaginative—but completely asinine—names for them. Have you ever heard of "antidive geometry"? No, it is not a competitive diving strategy. It is a technology Mercedes installs in their cars. Peugeot has countered with its strut-style chassis. And, to take another nice example, perhaps Clorox's Oxi Magic laundry detergent will cut through the advertising clutter, though OxiClean may yet be the market leader in oxygen-based cleaners.

Headache tablets are drugs. Drugs always have a negative connotation because one associates them with illness, pains—and especially with chemistry. However, one manufacturer of headache tablets, Dolormin, uses stimulants equivalent to bodily substances, a fact that should ease the minds—and heads—of even the most hostile critics of the chemical industry.

In this concentrated form, the absurdity of this pseudoscientific gobbledygook in advertising is particularly glaring. But plenty of consumers are no longer able to laugh about so much nonsense. They feel annoyed and taken in.

Scenes are frequently depicted in advertising that have nothing to do with reality. In a commercial by Fairy Ultra set at a children's birthday party, children are shown sitting at a table with totally dirty, sticky plates. It is fair enough to ask how it is possible to keep an entire horde of children sitting at the table for days at a time. It must have been a matter of days because the fork that is shown is stuck so tightly to the plate that when the fork is raised the plate comes right off the table along with it. Or have the children perhaps been eating glue? The housewife's advice-giving mother, who of course always has a packet of said dishwashing powder at hand, is emptying equally dirty *wine glasses* (!) out of the dishwasher. What had they been doing? Using alcohol to keep the children quiet for days on end with their dirty plates in front of them?

In some detergent ads, the dirty clothes are so filthy that the dirt probably couldn't be removed even with hydrochloric acid. But the advertising strategists of the washing machine manufacturers apparently believe that there are indeed housewives who believe this nonsense.

How can an advertisement be good if it annoys the people at whom it is directed?

Anyone who followed the rules of communicational marketing would not make mistakes like these. He or she would make sure to check the presentation at the relational level—beforehand.

Chapter 22
The Facts in Advertising, the Statistics

In the strategy of feigned competence described in the preceding chapter, the expert or the socially well-defined, competent role model (father, mother, doctor, mountaineer, clergyperson, auto mechanic, politician, manager, captain of industry) is ascribed a high degree of competence in some particular area. The truth thereby becomes reduced to the way a certain expert sees it. Then the question is who is acknowledged as an expert. Ultimately, it is a person who is considered to be an expert by another person. This leads to endless relativity. But the more fundamental question is why do so-called "facts" play such a dominant role in psychological marketing in the first place?

Many marketing decisions are based on statistical comparisons. Statistical comparisons are looked upon as proof. This is understandable, because the thinking is that numbers always sound convincing—particularly when they are not immediately verifiable and the listener is inclined to accept figures "just like that."

I am acquainted with a highly successful junior manager who works in sales for an international paper corporation. When I made a remark about the pointlessness of long statistical lectures overloaded with figures, he gave the following response: "If a person has achieved the best results in the high-quality paper sector of the company and has built up the most functional and hardest hitting sales team, then it must be permissible to describe these successes sometime!"

Since I know this young manager personally and value him a great deal, I broke off the attempt to convince him that a presentation flooded with facts would probably lead to the opposite of what he intended. It doesn't make any great difference whether one is trying to get across a point of view or an advertising plug. If you overload your message with "facts," then you always run the risk that the addressee will switch off at some point—either because he doesn't understand anything anymore or because your information makes you suspect—for the impression can arise that you want to cover something up with such a profusion of scarcely intelligible or unverifiable "facts."

Psychologically oriented marketing experts seem to assume that they imbibe the truth in the morning at breakfast and can then use it as a panacea to cure consumers of their wrong-headed frames of reference. Whoever puts facts at the center of their observations and assessments earnestly believes in an objective reality. The consequences are product fetishism (when a producer falls in love with its own product), misjudgment of consumer behavior, and the waste of million-dollar budgets that could be used for worthwhile things.

Psychological marketing will never succeed in getting customers to change their opinions. Once formed, convictions, opinions, and points of view can be corrected only with great difficulty. It seems to be part of human nature to orient oneself in terms of one's experiences, be they ever so limited and superficial. If the consumer has had even the slightest experience with a product or a product category, this product or category will already have been assigned a place in the consumer's frame of reference. That means that consumers are right as far as they are concerned. It is precisely the notions that exist only in the mental sphere that are so tenaciously accepted as truth.

An idea that exists only in the mind is usually viewed as the real truth. It is extremely seldom that people admit mistakes to themselves, and hardly ever to others. The incautious admission of errors and mistakes could signal weakness, which would then collide with the principle mechanisms of an achievement-and success-oriented society.

Perceptions, frames of reference, and the resulting worldviews are stronger than factual arguments and much stronger than the products themselves.

It is not the objective facts that decide the marketing battles among automobile manufacturers—facts like horsepower, traction, or equipment (windshield wipers that press against the windshield at higher speeds or an underside airbag that lifts the car up over the danger zone at an impending accident). The main factor in selling is the impression that buyers have of brands and the images associated with them. Maybe you can imagine a four-door Ferrari or, even better, a Ferrari station wagon. What about a Ferrari ATV? The notion of a Ferrari van or dump truck will stretch your fantasy to the absolute limit. But, okay, all is possible. Porsche was very successful with his Cayenne.

Marketing means approaching and dealing with the mind-sets of consumers in the most sensitive way possible. To diversify by trying to dance at a lot of different parties at once is not only an expensive and wasteful game, it is also a most definitely *anticommunicative* one.

The fact that the success of a product depends on the subjective value systems of the potential customers is clearly visible in the sales figures of international manufacturers. Some products that stand out as the absolute leaders of the pack do so only in certain countries. In other countries, they can't seem to get off the starting block. This is true in spite of completely identical "facts": the same qualities, the same advertising budgets, the same market conditions, the same target-group orientation. If the much ballyhooed power of products really did reside in the products themselves, then all products ought to sell equally well or poorly all over the world.

Heinz soup has met with tremendous success in Great Britain. In Germany, on the other hand, it hasn't been able to assert itself against Knorr and Maggi. From a communicational perspective, the reason is no mystery: in Germany, "Heinz" means "ketchup" and that's the end of the story. Markets are just simply not psychological laboratories.

The question posed earlier about objective truth is thereby answered. Philosophers of antiquity, as well as those of the modern era, have long established that truth cannot be objective. Why should it of all places be marketing where this insight does *not* hold true? Perhaps at some point someone will, in her divine wisdom, discover the objective truth somewhere. But it won't be in marketing.

Chapter 23

Communicational Marketing Within the Organization

Intra-Company Communication

We now turn to "internal" communication. The term *internal* has been put in quotation marks because in the understanding of communicational marketing there is no such thing as internal communication in the sense of communication that takes place *exclusively* within a company.

Communicational marketing starts from the premise of the interrelatedness of all company communication—whether it be communication among employees or between employees and management, within the organizational structure, or whatever. Communication affects and is affected by everything: the overall ambiance, the behavior of executives toward one another, the existing hierarchies—in short, everything from the choice and care of the fleet of vehicles to the company philosophy.

While considering these relationships, the impossibility of *not* communicating should be kept in mind. Regardless of how trivial or insignificant it might seem, everything is constantly affecting the behavior of the individual and the group, and ultimately the behavior of the customer toward the company.

In the first two parts of this book, you no doubt recognized situations similar to ones you have experienced and that you can now better understand with the knowledge of communicational rules. It was made clear how innumerable the factors are upon which communication depends.

It would be beyond the scope of any discussion to try to identify and interpret the ramifications of all these seemingly endless and sometimes subtle influences on everything we say and do. *Communicational marketing does not require the analysis of all possible factors influencing human behavior. But it does urgently warn against ignoring them.*

Communicational Quality

In the 1980s, numerous American companies were analyzed by Tom Peters and Robert Waterman, two American efficiency experts with the consulting firm McKinsey & Co. The two consultants were particularly interested in finding out whether essential common elements could be identified in leadership, strategy, product management, and organization. They interviewed managers at companies, such as IBM, Hewlett Packard, Procter & Gamble, McDonald's, Coca-Cola, and many more, and then compiled their findings in their 1984 book *In Search of Excellence: Lessons from America's Best Companies.*[23] Some of their discoveries are of particular interest from the communicational point of view.

The consultants came to the realization that in order to build up new strength in a company it is not enough simply to know its weaknesses. Now, everyone who has completed a course of studies in classic economics can confirm the fact that the primary emphasis in this discipline is put on avoiding or eliminating possible weaknesses (attainment of the highest degree of efficiency and effectiveness by means of profit maximization and cost minimization; the economic principle in operation is highest possible profit with the lowest possible resource utilization). Academic economics as well as business training courses are concerned mainly with *problems* and their avoidance. This approach, which is solidly based on economic principles, has firmly established itself in everyday business life. As soon as supply shortages or any kind of problems or mistakes—financial or ideational—arise anywhere, an intensive search for causes, i.e., weaknesses, immediately gets under way.

The result of a company analysis by a traditional management consultant, who does not think in communicational concepts, consists of interminably long lists of mistakes, deficiencies, false investment decisions, etc. This result frequently concludes with the recommendation to dismiss at least 10% of the company workforce for being unmotivated or stupid or for not working to capacity.

The only explanation for this consultancy practice seems to be the circumstance that such analyses can be easily "documented" with nicely colored charts. The concentration on and search for mathematically determinable, measurable, and calculable indications in business consultancy

---

23   Peters, Tom, and Robert Waterman. *In Search of Excellence.* Verlag moderne industrie AG, 1984.

praxis is a carry-over from the compulsion at schools and universities to make performances uniformly measurable—i.e., *testable*.

But the leadership qualities of a future manager depend less on her mathematical tabulation skills than on her communication skills. How communication works, however, is not taught at universities to economics or business students, apart from perhaps some smatterings of information that might be offered in elective rhetoric workshops. These, however, usually deal more with the psychological aspects of rhetoric than with the communicational aspects.

Given the ramifications of the communicational aspects described here, it seems reasonable that not only marketing, with its outward orientation, but also the success of a company as a whole depends decisively on the intercommunicational patterns and dynamics within it. Where is the management consultant to be found who examines the communicational requirements of the company that hires him or her to do an analysis? If the company in its totality is viewed as a communication pool, then it seems that the informational aspects (numbers, sales volume, profit, quantities) are the only ones that get evaluated with traditional procedures. The relational aspects are simply ignored. Hence no metacommunication takes place, for this type of procedure involves precisely these relational aspects. But metacommunication is particularly important for identifying the punctuation (see chapters 4 and 13) of the various intercommunicational patterns in the first place.

Intra-company communicational marketing proceeds in a different manner. Instead of inflexibly searching for *weaknesses*, the emphasis is put on the *strengths* of the company. If one asks an entrepreneur how his or her company is doing, one often hears the answer that the company is doing quite well, but "the personnel ..., the suppliers ..., the constantly unsatisfied customers ..., the banks ..." Problems are at the center of the communicational frame of reference. This means negativity. It is the same type of negativity that was already developed in the frames of reference and worldviews at schools and universities.

Whoever is familiar with the tenacious, self-perpetuating nature of communicational frames of reference also knows that, once established, it is almost impossible to overturn these mind-sets. However, many manager seminars embark on just this dicey venture in the apparently boundless faith in the power of the psychology. Every direct attempt on the part of a manager to talk an employee into having a more positive worldview will give the employee the feeling of being under attack—a frontal attack on his or her frame of reference. This kind of pep talk ("Let's try to think and act positively!") takes place at the relational level and constitutes a typical "Be spontaneous!" paradox. This paradox now automatically sets in motion the communicational mechanism of the CIP Pyramid as explained in chapter 9.

Peters and Waterman paid particularly close attention to those factors that functioned well in spite of structures that were objectively—in the classic economic sense of the word—inadequate. The two consultants found out that there is one capability that distinguishes all successful companies alike: all innovative, successful companies have the ability to adapt to every change in their environment, certain bombastic structures notwithstanding. Successful companies have all developed their own individual strategies for changing with great rapidity when the environment changes. Most miscarriages could be traced back to the failure to make the necessary changes or to make them in time.

These companies carefully register all relevant factors—shifts in customers' needs, increases in the efficiency of competitors, their public image, ecological considerations, changes in government regulations and political power constellations—and adapt to each new state of affairs. In these companies, managerial instruments hadn't supplanted thinking. Analytical methods had not impeded activity. On the contrary, the attempt was always made to present even complex constellations and relationships in the simplest possible manner. These top companies treated their employees like adults. They developed champions for innovative products and service. A certain degree of chaos was tolerated if it facilitated faster and less complicated courses of action.

Peters and Waterman learned that the most successful companies don't hesitate to get things going. The proof of the pudding is in the eating. To be sure, outstanding companies do make use of analysis and analytic methods; but this is not where the main emphasis lies. This shift of emphasis reduces the risk of dissipating energies, for whoever concentrates too long on the question of methodology will lose sight of the real objectives. Methodological discussions lead to endlessly repetitive meetings devoid of content which come to nothing in the end. Effective intra-company communication should create possibilities and not impediments for the free flow of ideas. Theory-laden communication obstructionists are no use to anyone. Just one self-glorifying antipragmatist can endanger the entire effectiveness of a highly creative team. Eagerness to experiment and the courage to try out new things—that is what is called for in a technological age advancing at breathtaking speed.

Particularly major corporations have to fight constantly against inertia. In most big companies, there is the entrenched attitude that since everything is so big already, everything can only get slower. If the management itself is already communicating this bureaucratic attitude, where are the highly motivated employees supposed to come from who want to get things going?

For this size-related sluggishness, solutions should be developed with the kind of dynamic and flexibility that gives small- and medium-sized companies their strength.

Peters and Waterman also found that "the best companies learn from their customers. They offer incomparable quality, service, and reliability, plus durable products that run smoothly. They succeed in giving a touch of class to even the most run-of-the-mill, mass-produced article. Many innovative companies owe their best product ideas to their customers. This is the payoff for constant, attentive listening."

This sounds simple. But learning from customers means communicating with them—actively. Take advantage of every opportunity to get an opinion. Don't ask your product managers or your engineers. Ask the consumer.

It's the dream of every entrepreneur that all employees think the way the boss does. This would clearly be the ideal situation. But this state of affairs cannot be attained by simply postulating it. In the communicational understanding, to explicitly require entrepreneurial thinking from your employees is to demand spontaneous behavior. Give them spheres of action and initiative instead, and they will respond accordingly.

The report on 3M states that the people there are so obsessed with innovation that the general atmosphere reminds one less of a large-scale enterprise and more of a maze of laboratories and cubbyholes in which eager inventors and intrepid entrepreneurs give full scope to their imagination. Not every company has the means and possibilities of 3M. But even smaller companies can find ways to delegate responsibility that go beyond the autonomous administration of stamps and paper clips. The risk of increasing the rate of error by delegating responsibility is ridiculously low compared with the advantage of having active, company-oriented employees. It ought to be worth an attempt. Give it a try.

Don't analyze the psychology of your employees. You will never be able to figure it out anyway, let alone influence it. Analyze your intra-company communication instead—the relational aspects and the pattern of interaction.

When problems do arise, this is often due to the pattern of communication and not to the factual issues involved. When there is a stalemate—as for example in classic conflicts between executives and employees—solutions cannot be found at the factual level. The ability to metacommunicate shifts the situation onto a new, overarching level. From this perspective, the initial deadlock is much easier to overcome.

Strive for communicational transparency in your role as executive. If in critical situations you succeed in getting people in your company to talk about communication itself, a new kind of openness—without artificiality—

will come about. This openness doesn't result from the call for spontaneous behavior ("Be open to one another!"), which never works anyway; it emerges spontaneously on its own.

Especially nowadays, in the multimedia age, the new type of modern manager is an expert on communication!

Chapter 24
Personal Communicational Marketing: An Example

Communicational Influencing

Whether in private or professional life, everyone wants to influence others in some way. There are all kinds of reasons for this: to change the behavior of our partners, bring up children, develop new business contacts, motivate employees, take care of customers, or maintain friendships. Whatever the motivations for your actions toward others are, the underlying aim is always to influence their behavior.

As we have learned from the axioms of communication, even the supposedly straightforward statement that one doesn't want to influence others is simply another attempt to do just that, no matter how one tries to get around it. We exist; therefore, we communicate.

Regardless of what we try to communicate, it is up to the recipient to decide how he or she wants to interpret it. It follows from this that our statements and gestures can be interpreted *falsely*. The other party can accept our communications, ignore them, or turn them into the opposite. At the relational level, nothing is impossible.

A question certainly worth asking is whether there are any possibilities of influencing others without manipulating them. How can we influence others without transgressing the bounds of ethical principles?

If you have internalized the laws of human communication, you have a very powerful tool at your disposal. *The basic idea of communicational marketing is to analyze how any statement could be understood by the addressee before making it.* This doesn't mean simply saying what people want to hear. This behavior is easy to see through and can bring about just the opposite of what you are trying to accomplish.

In order to put communicational marketing into practice, you have to adopt a somewhat complicated—but very effective—three-step rhetorical approach. We shall demonstrate these three steps or phases with the example of a sales talk.

Phase 1: The Basic Issue

If one presupposes a competent dialogue partner who doesn't simply accept everything like a sheep being led to the slaughter, then to influence her you must convince her. In order to convince the other party of your idea, your product, or your performance, you first need information.

If you don't know her point of view, her frame of reference, then you have no possibility of confirming it, let alone changing it. You will be groping around in the dark. With a head-on, digital attack, you stand a fifty-fifty chance of falling flat on your face—which also means you have a fifty-fifty chance of succeeding.

Therefore, the first step is to find out what your dialogue partner really thinks and where she stands with respect to specific points before making any objective offer (digital message). This is not easy. If the other party becomes aware of being interviewed, she could interpret your questions as already constituting an attack. For this reason, the answers should be elicited and interpreted at the relational level.

Remember that what counts is not what is said but how the other party understands what is said. In the case of a sales talk with a customer, we move up to a more complex communication level: what is of interest here is not only how our input is received by the customer, but also the effect of customer feedback on us.

Let's take an example. We are selling some kind of machine. The general criteria for purchasing decisions with respect to machinery are quickly listed: quality, speed of operation, longevity, fast and inexpensive provision of spare parts, low maintenance costs, low energy consumption, ecological considerations, noise, good and fast service from the supplier, and price.

Everyday experience shows that customers set very definite priorities for their buying decisions. These priorities can be compared with the product ladder described earlier. It might be the price that tops the list for one customer. Perhaps the buyer of the machine has his own service team and doesn't require further support. For someone else, the ecological and safety aspects of the machine are of primary interest. You might be lucky and have a customer who responds straightaway to the direct question of what the most important characteristics for him are. But even if he tells you in straightforward manner what his priorities are, and you promptly confirm these by recommending your product, you could still have fallen into a communication trap: this confirmation was made at the informational level, and this is a level that plays hardly any role in communication. In other words, although you have confirmed your customer, he will assume that this confirmation was just made out of pure self-interest anyway and not in order to offer him a genuine solution.

The art of finding out what interests your customer most (i.e., what the most important consideration for his purchasing decision is)—this art consists in finding out the answer at the relational level and not at the informational level.

Phase 2: Induced Dominance

Let us assume that you were able to find out by means of metacommunicational interpretation what the most important factor is for your customer. This factor should now be made the topic of conversation. If the main emphasis of the prospective buyer is not on one of the criteria listed above, but rather on something unexpected like aesthetic considerations, this is what should now be talked about.

The greatest mistake at this point would consist in saying to the customer, who is perhaps interested in elegant machines with a modern design, something like, "We build the most beautiful, the most colorful, the most aesthetic machines in the entire world!" What you should do at this stage is express your interest in aesthetics in general. Search for an area of agreement that doesn't have anything to do with your product—and absolutely nothing to do with your desire to sell. Perhaps, in the case of another customer you discovered at some point that this person was interested in a good price and nothing else. At this point, it would be premature to immediately point out how reasonably priced your own offers are.

The point of establishing common ground is to get on the same wavelength. By so doing, you maneuver yourself consciously into a supporting role and assign the leading role to the other party. This gives the other person the security of feeling that he or she is the one making the decisions, controlling the course of the conversation, and hence not being manipulated.

Putting your communication partner in the (apparently) dominant position is a simple matter. Advance an opinion, for example, that you know from the start that your customer will refute. After he or she has made their case, agree (gratefully) and add that you had never considered the matter from that point of view before. And thereby your customer already dominates the exchange (from his point of view).

Another possibility is to ask the other person a factual question that you are pretty sure he can answer with ease. Try to ask the question in such a way that the answer is delivered in a lecturing, perhaps even arrogant manner. Then you have won. The customer dominates the interaction (from his point of view).

Phase 3: Indirect Confirmation

The confirmation should take place only after it is perfectly clear what the customer's priorities for a buying decision are. The effectiveness of the confirmation depends decisively on whether it is communicated directly at the informational level ("Our machines are particularly reliable!") or within the context of a relational message.

Keep in mind that messages communicated at the relational level are always the result of individual feelings. A judgment made or an opinion formed at this level is entirely the result of the recipient's own thought processes and therefore "truth." And what's truth for her is *your* truth, period. The course of the interaction is reinforced by the dominant role you assigned to the other party in Phase Two.

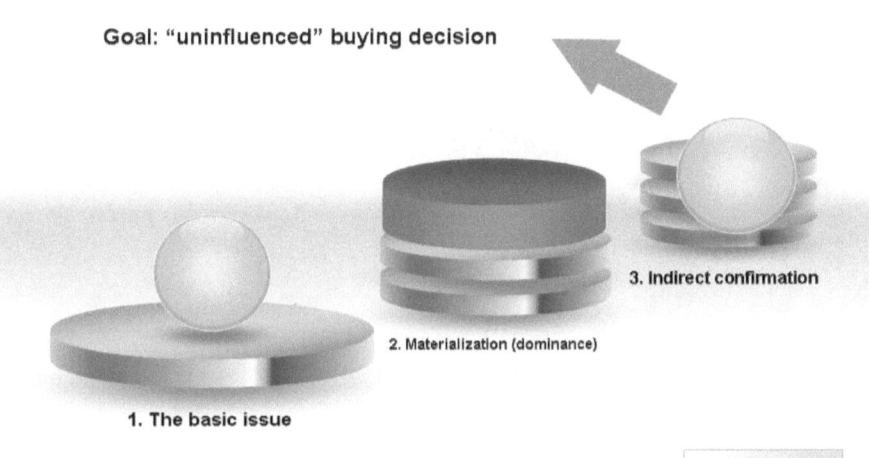

Rhetorical Influencing

Goal: "uninfluenced" buying decision

3. Indirect confirmation

2. Materialization (dominance)

1. The basic issue

COMMUNICATIONAL MARKETING

In our attempts to exert influence on other persons, we run the risk of making three great mistakes. All of them are connected with the fact of ignoring the relational aspects of communication.

Mistake No. 1: We give advice before we have thoroughly understood the other person. Understanding should be completed prior to handing out advice. It constitutes the key to every successful attempt to influence. If we don't understand the other person, if we don't put ourselves in her position, we cannot possibly provide adequate advice. What is more, since she will already feel under attack by this lack of empathy, we will learn nothing about any possible available gaps in her communicational frame of reference.

Mistake No. 2: We try to build up relationships without changing our own attitudes and behavior. No technique along the lines of the motto "Win friends!" will work if others experience us as self-contradictory. Trust is built up on the basis of lived continuity. Principles can be of help here.

Mistake No. 3: We start out from the assumption that it is enough "to set a good example." We think that our good example speaks for itself and therefore we forgo further explanations and instructions. In the final analysis, however, what we are communicates itself much more clearly and convincingly than what we say or even what we do.

Chapter 25

The Interaction Blueprint for Communicational Marketing

As an aid for the analysis of the communicational aspects of your marketing endeavors, some criteria are summarized here in this interaction blueprint. Place this "stencil" over your marketing strategy. If less than 50% of the indicators apply, then your plan of action is in need of communicational correction.

"Do you know your communication patterns, your company, your products, your employees, and your customers?" *In my experience, entrepreneurs and executives in all branches and in all companies large and small invariably give the same answer to this question: "Of course I know my business!"* The heads of marketing departments even tend to react a little indignantly to my earnestly intended question. After all, they say, vast sums are expended for this purpose on analyses, personnel consultants, and market research. Where could there be a problem? Unfortunately, however, in most cases closer examination reveals that only very superficial information has been procured by these means.

Some interesting aspects may come to light by comparing the factors identified in this section with your own situation. Remember that the significance of the factual content of any communication becomes entirely secondary if the addressee is prepared to believe in its truth. This readiness arises when the information provided fits into the recipient's worldview, or frame of reference, thus confirming the rightness of his or her opinions. The best way to win the hearts and minds of consumers is to give them incentives to modify their respective frames of reference on their own terms and not to try to sell them on your opinions and worldview. Potential buyers should form their own opinions about products and make their own buying decisions. Views that develop as a result of their own thought processes are what constitute truth for them.

Do You Know Your Strengths?

The classic science of business administration deals primarily with the *weaknesses* of a company. The result is the allocation of important additional resources to the elimination of these weaknesses, instead of concentrating efforts on reinforcing and improving *strengths*. A company that is too preoccupied with its weaknesses also runs the risk of *signaling* weakness ("We're working on that!"). In order to be able to concentrate on strengths, however, you have to know them—and know them well. But watch out for exaggerations, such as, "We are the biggest, we are the best." The communicationally competent customer will register such pompous slogans with a tired smile.

Do You Know Your Target Group?

"Of course! Our target group consists of bright females, fourteen to seventeen years young, who use in-line skates!"

Wonderful! But how do you go about identifying the target group's frame of reference? Is there a uniform frame of reference in the first place? Does your offer or your product mesh with the frame or frames of reference of your target group, or just with the "objective" characteristics of the target-group description? Learn to recognize the difference!

Do You Know Your Present Position?

What position does your company occupy in the opinion of the consumer? Has any attempt been made to determine it? Do you have any benchmark methods? What position do you think your product occupies in consumers' frames of reference? On which rung of the product ladder do you stand? Where might there gaps that need to be filled? Are you perhaps already proclaiming a position to your customers that you have yet to attain?

If you do not know where you stand with the consumer, then any statement made to this effect in your elegant company brochures belongs in the realm of legends and old wives' tales—regardless of how subjectively convinced you might be of its truth. Merely speculating about this point also makes it extraordinarily difficult for you to fight the competition, for you cannot really know anything about it! Only when you know your own present position can you determine the position just above you (the competitor who is beating you at present) and the one just below you (your hottest pursuer!). One of the greatest strengths of the Prussian military commander Clausewitz was his precise assessment of his opponents.

Are You Credible or Do You Just Want to Be?

Check where in your company credibility is asserted and trust is asked for, perhaps even demanded. Whoever asserts their credibility is in urgent need of it (remember the CIP Pyramid). It is much better simply to *be* credible. However, this is the end result of a long process in which every company has to first establish its credibility. Do not demand trust, communicate it!

Is the Attempt Being Made to Not Communicate?

Check the way complaints are handled. This is an ideal area for the attempt to avoid communication. A cardinal error can be observed repeatedly. The first reaction to a customer complaint is to cast doubt on it. "You say the machine doesn't run? That can't be true!" This situation calls for cooperation and not attack. You should express your gratitude for complaints, for the easiest alternative to a complaint is the switch to your competitor. And you can well imagine how many other customers one dissatisfied customer takes with her.

Who Is at the Center of Your Communication?

Count the number of times you use the words "I," "we," "my," "our" in your correspondence. In telephone conversations, one also tends to put oneself in the center. Recall that recipients are primarily interested in their own affairs. Therefore, put the other person in the center of the communication—rhetorically as well. Instead of saying "I will send you our documents shortly," for example, say "You will soon receive the material!"

Are Your Customers Competent?

The factual-informational level of your advertising statements is normally pretty straightforward: "With our detergent, you can now wash even whiter!" But what about the relational level? How is the message coming across to the consumer? This alone is what counts! If your advertising message accords your potential customers no intelligence and no competence, there is little probability that they will be attracted to your product.

Or what is your opinion of people who think you're stupid?

Do You Communicate about Communication?

Metacommunication is the high road to successful communication. The absence of metacommunication is like trying to learn a foreign language by boning up on vocabulary and leaving out grammar entirely. You will stammer out strings of words along the grammatical lines of your own language. Although the attentive listener will understand some of what you say, misunderstandings are programmed in from the start.

Communication problems arise in a similar manner. The parties involved are unable to agree on grammar. This shouldn't happen to you when you develop your next advertising conception. Learn the grammar of your potential customers—i.e., learn how they communicate, how they understand messages in advertisements—beforehand.

How Do "Problems" Get Solved?

In any given situation, first check to see whether there is really a problem at all. Many problems can be traced back to all the various and often highly individual ways people have of communicating; much of this stems from widespread disagreement on grammar. The failure to recognize this circumstance creates the problem in the first place. The issue is often not a problem at all but only a minor difficulty that each party simply prefers to solve with a different form of communication.

It is a good idea to adopt the following attitude, one which has often helped me to prevent such conflicts. *There are no major problems, only unsolved minor difficulties.*

When difficulties arise transcend your own frame of reference. Move onto a higher communicational plane from which you can get a broad overview of the entire communicational situation. At this level, solutions will suddenly become visible.

Do You Keep Tabs on Interactions?

You will recall that every communication is subject to a certain pattern of interaction. Communication can take place complementarily or symmetrically. It is not an easy task but a very helpful one if you make it a habit to keep tabs on the course of interactions. Ideally, you will become aware of your position in any given instance of communication. Become your own communication manager.

Do You Make Clear What You're Asking of Customers?

Classical marketing largely involves the formulation of utility-oriented advertising statements. The advantages of your product over that of direct competitors, other types of products, and service offerings are determined with the greatest precision (object level of the communication) and presented by means of the most modern advertising techniques. From the communicational perspective, this is perfectly in order.

But what about the relational level? This level invariably contains—if advertising is involved in any way at all—an enjoinment to buy. ("Buy our product, because we are better, faster, higher, longer, more reasonably priced.") Oftentimes these enjoinments are not explicitly formulated in agency presentations. This is perhaps due to fears that clearly formulated directives could be felt to be presumptuous. (As an example, see the McDonald's "I'm lovin' it!" campaign.) This attitude is not only false but is also an instance of unpardonable neglect of communicational realities. The analysis of enjoinments in advertising messages can, in fact, lead to astonishing results. At a brainstorming session, it is advisable to bring in uninterested third parties to check new ideas against consumers' relational reality.

Formulate your enjoinments clearly before you unleash your advertising messages on your customers! Remember that *every* advertising message contains an enjoinment at the relational level!

An analysis of the communicational effect at the relational level requires a discussion of the number and variety of demands connected with advertising messages. It can be determined, for example, if advertising messages contain "Be spontaneous!" paradoxes or enjoinments that create double binds.

Once again, it is not *what* is communicated to the recipient that counts, but *how* it is received.

Are You Aware of the Power Structures in Your Company?

No matter how modern, streamlined, and liberal it otherwise is, every company contains power structures. What makes power suspect is the fact that it doesn't have to be actively created. Nor does power have to manifest itself in demagogy or oppressive agitation. It is simply there, brought about by organizational forms, sociocultural structures, or mere force of habit.

As long as it is not abused, power is not a problem in and of itself. But denying the existence of actual power structures does create problems. Then power takes on an unpredictable, threatening, and dangerous aspect. Therefore the existence of power should not be denied.

Do You Try to Change People?

An old Chinese proverb says, "You can change mountains and rivers but never people." Nevertheless, I think that everyone, intentionally or not, does their fair share daily to change their fellow human beings in one way or another. Who or what shapes current events if not human beings? If no changes came about, ethnologically and socially we would still be standing today where we were at the beginning of our developmental history. The truly remarkable, key experiences which influence our behavior, or even transform it entirely, originate with other people. We perceive and register the behavior of others. However, whether we accept it or even adopt it depends on whether it is compatible with our frames of reference.

People cannot be changed (up to this point, the wise Chinese were right) by a direct attack on their frame of reference. They will immediately react with an aggressive or defensive stance without stopping to examine your objection or your proposal. To achieve changes it is important to know the frame of reference in question before inducing your dialogue partner to reexamine their reference system or perhaps even reorganize it. The new opinion or mind-set you want to communicate has to be the result of your dialogue partner's own process of reflection on his or her own frame of reference. In this way, your partner forms an own opinion. And this opinion is always right.

Do Your Employees Know How Communication Works?

Behavior toward customers, colleagues, and superiors is an unending source of material for discussion. If lasting, positive changes in behavior are to be effected, this will function substantially better and faster if those involved know how communication works. Explain it to them, or even better, have it explained to them by third parties (in seminars and in-house training courses).

The provision of service in many companies does not size up particularly well, especially in retailing. And as mundane as it might sound, this also holds true for the friendliness of the personnel. And this despite the fact that friendliness is a top priority for many consumers evaluating business enterprises!

However, to require friendliness ("Try to be a little friendlier..."), is a perfect example of the "Be spontaneous!" paradox. In all probability, the expression of this wish would lead to just the opposite behavior. If employees know how communication works, however, they are better able to evaluate themselves and their own forms of communication. They can then make a better assessment of the consequences of *their own* behavior on the behavior in their environment.

THE AUTHOR

Luigi Carlo De Micco is internationally active as a consultant, with focal points in communication, branding/brand-name creation, IT, financing and capital market transactions. De Micco & Friends (www.demicco.de) is a group of private, international and highly experienced entrepreneurs, who are active with investments and capital market transactions in a variety of segments.

CONSULTING SERVICES
Temporary leader

The very individual consulting concept of De Micco is not directed towards developing extensive, theoretical guides or business simulations. Instead it focuses on the development and implementation of practical measures for achieving the objectives of the entrepreneur. As a part of his consultancy assignments, De Micco makes himself available as a "temporary leader", for implementing the desired objectives in a hands-on manner. Depending on the mission, a well-trained management team can be made available. The objective is not only consulting, analysing, creating concepts and planning, but the actual "doing".

Medium-sized companies, internationally active enterprises of the IT and the luxury goods industry, entrepreneurs and executives of international groups in Europe, USA, Asia and Latin America and politicians in leadership positions, can be found among the clients.

Institutional investors, such as investment banks, private equity companies, capital markets funds or venture capital companies, are using the many years of entrepreneurial experience gained by De Micco, in evaluating potential investments, assessing restructuring or portfolio realignment measures and mergers & acquisitions transactions. An individual sales or participation concept is developed for sellers of companies or participations.

CONSULTANT FOR GOVERNMENTS AND INSTITUTIONS

As a consultant of governments and institutions, De Micco is available for the development of strategic and tactical concepts, election campaigns and, as a representative and negotiating diplomat, for special missions related to bilateral relations.

De Micco represents the interface between companies and decision makers in governments and institutions, for international investments or market entries. He never acts as a mediator in international investment projects, only has a pure consultant. A commission for the successful conclusion of projects is never charged to the company or institutions making investments, nor to governments or their representatives.

De Micco & Friends INDUSTRY INVESTMENTS
Investments in entrepreneurs

De Micco & Friends invests internationally in a wide variety of industrial sectors. Besides a good product, a good communications strategy and an interesting market, each investment decision always focuses on the entrepreneur and his management team.

In addition to providing consultancy services on its own investments, De Micco & Friends also counsels private and institutional investors. Medium-sized companies, internationally active enterprises of the IT and the luxury goods industry, as well as entrepreneurs and executives of international groups in Europe, USA, Asia and Latin America can be found among our clients.

De Micco & Friends is not an institutional investor. It is a private and independent group of investors that makes private investments. The group manages exclusively it own, private financial resources; third-party capital is not taken up. In almost all investment that are made, the corresponding projects are supported operationally.

INVESTMENT COUNSELLING AND TRANSACTION HANDLING

Institutional investors, such as capital market funds or venture capital companies, use the many years of experience of De Micco and his team to assess new, potential investments, or to evaluate restructuring and portfolio realignments measures.

MERGERS & ACQUISITIONS

De Micco & Friends acts as a lead consultant in international M&A transactions, managing and organising such transactions for institutional investors and companies, both on the buyer and the seller side. For interested buyers of companies, and offerors of strategic participations or joint ventures, a targeted search and an analysis is made of suitable candidates, after which their acquisition is prepared.

An individual and informative sales and communications concept is developed for sellers of companies or offerors of participations. If not already available, De Micco & Friends will develop an informative sales or participation prospectus. Subsequently, potential International buyers and investors will be identified via the De Micco & Friends network, including other partners. The 75% closure rate for Merger & Acquisition transactions is above average. The duration of projects lies between 4 and 6 months.

LECTURES / PAPERS

Dr. De Micco is well known for his expert and interactive lectures, in which practical knowledge, and the professional know-how and experience of entrepreneurs, is not only presented in a competent manner for the areas of communications, branding and corporate financing, but also in an entertaining way.

On request, Dr. Luigi Carlo De Micco Is available for conferences, congresses, symposia, private special events and corporate events, if you would like to enrich your event with an exceptional speaker.

Contributions can be presented in German, English or Spanish.

www.ingramcontent.com/pod-product-compliance
Lightning Source LLC
Chambersburg PA
CBHW031056180526
45163CB00002BA/853